LIFE
ALONG
the LINE

A DAVID & CHARLES BOOK
Copyright © David & Charles Limited 2010

David & Charles is an F+W Media, Inc. company
4700 East Galbraith Road
Cincinnati, OH 45236

First published in the UK in 2010

Copyright © Paul Atterbury 2010

A catalogue record for this book is available from the British Library.

ISBN-13: 978-0-7153-3628-1
ISBN-10: 0-7153-3628-2

Printed in China by RR Donnelley
for David & Charles
Brunel House, Newton Abbot, Devon

Produced for David & Charles by
OutHouse Publishing
Winchester, Hampshire SO22 5DS

For OutHouse Publishing
Editor and Project Manager Sue Gordon
Art Editor Dawn Terrey
Proofreader Lindsey Brown
Indexer June Wilkins

For David & Charles
Commissioning Editor Neil Baber
Editor Verity Muir
Design Manager Sarah Clark
Production Controller Kelly Smith

Visit our website at www.davidandcharles.co.uk

For decades, country stations were at the centre of family and social life, and their closure affected thousands of ordinary lives. Typical was Caradog Falls Halt, on the line to Aberystwyth in West Wales, seen here in July 1964 as two women with a pram wait to board the local train to Aberystwyth.

LIFE
ALONG
the LINE

RAILWAYS AND PEOPLE

Paul Atterbury

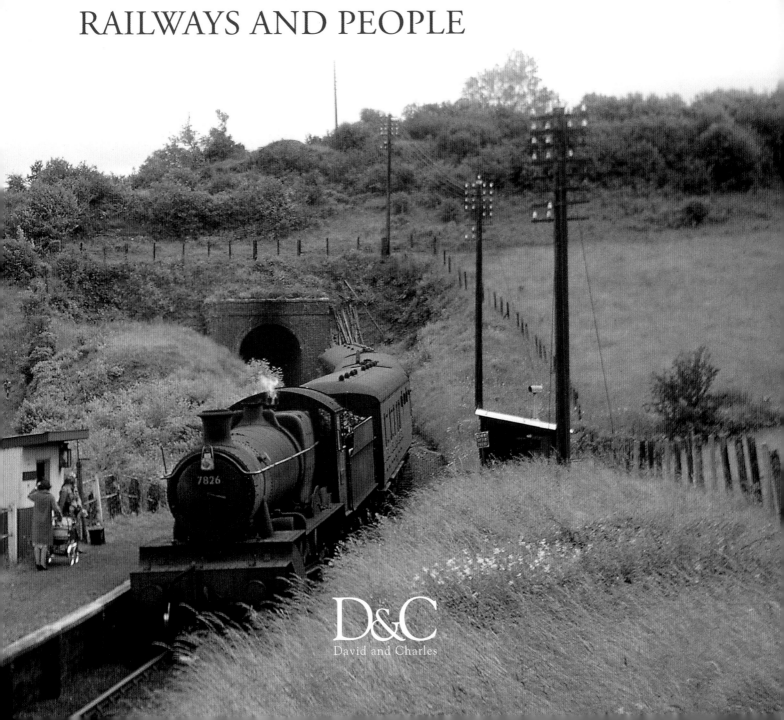

D&C

David and Charles

CONTENTS

➡ An elegant lady waits for a train while a porter goes about his work at an unidentified station in the Edwardian era.

➤ *A Midland Railway band poses before a Christmas concert in 1921 – a reflection of the all-encompassing nature of railway employment at that time.*

THE MIDLANDS HOLIDAY EXPRESS

Will Run
from

WOLVERHAMPTON (Low Level), BILSTON (Central),
WEDNESBURY (Central), WEST BROMWICH, and
BIRMINGHAM (Snow Hill)

FIRST WEEK   SECOND WEEK

MONDAY, 31st JULY   TUESDAY, 8th AUGUST
to   to
THURSDAY, 3rd August   FRIDAY, 11th August
                                  to
MONDAY - - - - WESTON-super-MARE   TUESDAY - - - - - - - - - RHYL
TUESDAY - - - - WINDSOR & RIVER   WEDNESDAY - LLANGOLLEN & TOUR
              THAMES CRUISE   THURSDAY - - - - LONDON & TOUR
WEDNESDAY - LLANGOLLEN & TOUR   FRIDAY - PORTSMOUTH & SOUTHSEA
THURSDAY - - - - - - - BLACKPOOL

FOUR DAYS' TRAVEL

INCLUSIVE 80/- EACH
FARE   WEEK

YOUR SEAT RESERVED IN A SPECIAL CAFETERIA CAR TRAIN
TO A DIFFERENT RESORT EACH DAY.
PASSENGERS MUST BOOK IN ADVANCE

BRITISH RAILWAYS   BJH.69

INTRODUCTION

The development of Britain's railway network during the 19th century completely changed the life of the nation. Travel became universally accessible, trade expanded, and cities, towns, villages and resorts flourished. Even the use of GMT throughout Britain came about as a result of the confusion caused by railway companies variously using London time and local time. The story of the railways is well documented, but frequently the people whose daily lives were at the heart of that story are overlooked. This book, based largely on photographs taken by amateurs (some of whom, unfortunately, did not note the date or location), offers a different view of Britain's railways by looking at the people who ran them, the people who used them, and the people who enjoyed them.

◆ Railways have always catered for leisure travel, and holiday excursions have been popular since the 1840s. Typical is this British Railways handbill of 1969 promoting the Midlands Holiday Express.

◆ On a wet day on a deserted platform in the 1970s a man, setting off on his own, perhaps for work, says goodbye to his wife and child. This familiar scene has always been part of railway travel. The setting is not identified, but the story is nonetheless important and has universal meaning.

◆ A smart Edwardian gentleman poses with his touring bicycle outside a GWR station. Cycling and the railway were natural partners, opening up possibilities of travel and exploration inconceivable before this period.

◆ The railways created the resorts and holiday regions of Britain. This is Dawlish, in South Devon, thronged with holidaymakers in 1950s fashions. All of them would have travelled here by train. Meanwhile a crowded express sets off for Cornwall.

Postcards from seaside resorts, such as this Edwardian example from Blackpool, were written by holidaymakers who had travelled by train, and it was trains that then carried the cards to their destinations. Some cards were published by railway companies.

A group of young men, perhaps staff or apprentices at a North Eastern Railway depot, pose on the side of a locomotive, in about 1900.

London Midland and Scottish Railway Company.
(2012 A)

ALL SEATS RESERVED

From _____ To _____

Train _____ Name _____

While the railways did not include cruise ships in their extensive maritime fleets, they did the next best thing by trying to bring a sense of leisure and relaxation into cross-Channel services. This brochure was issued in the early 1960s to promote a new ship, the SS *Falaise*, designed to make a routine voyage pleasurable and exciting.

IN THE DRIVER'S CAB

The train driver, a figure representing both romance and skilful dedication, often featured in railway publicity. This cigarette card shows a Southern Railway electric train driver, an image of modernity, efficiency and comfort far removed from the world of steam.

GUERNSEY
THE SUNSHINE ISLAND
SERVICES VIA WEYMOUTH OR SOUTHAMPTON
BY GREAT WESTERN OR SOUTHERN RAILWAYS
FOR OFFICIAL HANDBOOKS SEND 3D TO PUBLICITY MANAGER, STATES OFFICE, GUERNSEY

PA
THE FA
Guide 6

TR

IN AND AROUND
**THE WEST
COUNTRY**

GNTON SOUTH
DEVON

ILY RESORT OF PICTURESQUE TORBAY

from Dept. "P", Publicity Manager, Paignton

VEL BY TRAIN   BRITISH RAILWAYS

STATION SCENES

The railways of the Southwest were interestingly varied. The few main lines supported a dense network of rural routes and branch lines, and there were numerous small stations serving country towns and villages, many of which have closed since the 1950s. Traffic was mixed: passenger services were busy during the holiday season, while regular goods trains carried vegetables, fruit, flowers and other agricultural produce, minerals and local freight throughout the year. A number of coastal resorts in Cornwall, Devon and Dorset depended on the railways, both major West Country services, such as the daily Cornish Riviera and Atlantic Coast expresses to and from London, and the many local trains. A selection of stations in these counties, along with some in Somerset, feature on these pages.

▷ The line to Ilfracombe, a heavily graded 14-mile branch from Barnstaple, was opened in 1874 and in due course became one of the destinations for the Atlantic Coast Express. Here, in the 1960s, passengers disembark from the local stopping train while mailbags are loaded and unloaded.

▽ It is a quiet, hazy day in the summer of 1962 at Penzance. Two long trains await their passengers and a GWR Class 6800 locomotive, No. 6845, 'Paviland Grange', slowly backs towards some wagons.

▷ Steam and diesel meet at Torrington, on the Devon line south from Barnstaple Junction and Bideford. There seem to be no passengers, and closure, in 1965, is not far off. Today the station survives as a pub and the line is a cycle track.

▽ Petrockstow was one of a number of rural stations in North Devon, on the remote line from Torrington to Halwill Junction. Despite handsome stone buildings, there was never much traffic.

△ At Halwill the LSWR's meandering north Cornwall line met the branch to Bude and the line south from Torrington, to be seen branching away at the top of the photograph. Until the late 1950s this was a busy place, but little survives today.

◁ The sidings at Okehampton often saw military traffic, for exercises nearby. Here, at some point before World War I, horse teams are being assembled. The horses have been delivered to the station by train, together with men and equipment.

△ The impressive signal gantry at Southampton towers over West Country Class No. 34046, 'Braunton', as it takes water before hauling its express on to Weymouth in August 1965. The assorted onlookers include a railway enthusiast wearing, typically, a raincoat.

△ At Woody Bay, on the Lynton & Barnstaple Railway, the only sign of life on this wet day in the early 1930s is the stationmaster making his way across the tracks. No trains are due, so the photographer is allowed to stand on the line.

◁ While a man poses for the camera on Axminster's bay platform, a tank locomotive awaiting duties on the Lyme Regis branch lifts its safety valve. The water tower, LSWR station lamp and British Railways totem nameplate add period detail to the image.

▷ This Edwardian view shows Midsomer Norton station on the Somerset & Dorset Joint Railway. The decorative paintwork, milk churns ready for collection and ladies in smart hats off on a shopping trip or visiting friends, make a lively scene.

▽ Two men and a boy have adopted a deliberately casual pose at Moorswater, near Liskeard, the only passenger station on the clay line from Coombe to the quarries at Caradon and Cheesewring.

▽ At Weymouth in the 1950s the Channel Islands ferry has docked and the train is ready to depart along the quay tramway, with a Class 5700 tank engine in charge. Three men chat with the driver while, to the left, a couple are deep in conversation beside their elegant Triumph saloon.

13

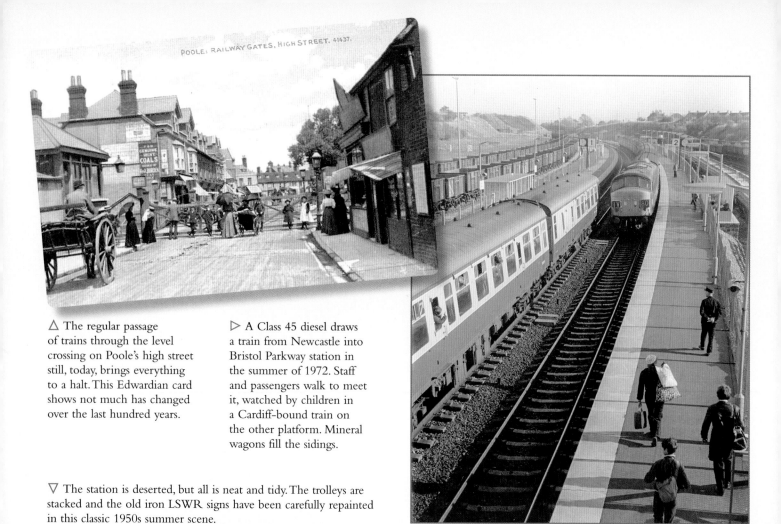

POOLE: RAILWAY GATES, HIGH STREET. 41437.

△ The regular passage of trains through the level crossing on Poole's high street still, today, brings everything to a halt. This Edwardian card shows not much has changed over the last hundred years.

▷ A Class 45 diesel draws a train from Newcastle into Bristol Parkway station in the summer of 1972. Staff and passengers walk to meet it, watched by children in a Cardiff-bound train on the other platform. Mineral wagons fill the sidings.

▽ The station is deserted, but all is neat and tidy. The trolleys are stacked and the old iron LSWR signs have been carefully repainted in this classic 1950s summer scene.

TICKET OFFICE

△ The Gothic style of Bristol Temple Meads makes it one of Britain's most distinctive stations. The typically Victorian blend of Tudor and French motifs in two-colour stone was designed by Matthew Digby Wyatt and completed in 1878. This photograph shows the building in 1973, soon after a full and careful restoration.

◁ A porter halts his passage across the tracks for the photographer in this moody view of Bristol Temple Meads, taken perhaps in the 1920s. Behind him, the 4-4-2 tank is ready to depart, and in the background the station walls are covered in advertisements.

△ This is Witham, a junction station in Somerset, on the line from Frome to Castle Cary, in 1956. The train from Yatton via Wells and Shepton Mallet has just arrived, the few passengers are making their way towards the exit, a trolley laden with milk crates waits on the platform – and a member of the station staff keeps his eye on the photographer.

▽ The branch from Congresbury along the Wrington Vale to Blagdon, in Somerset, was an early closure, with passenger traffic ending in 1931. Shortlived, it had opened in 1901, partly to help in the construction of a reservoir. Blagdon station survives as a private house, complete with benches, lamp and a brake-van body.

▷ Holt Junction, between Westbury and Chippenham, was the junction for the line to Devizes, part of a long-vanished rural Wiltshire network. The remote but substantial station, closed in 1968, had plenty of classic GWR details, including lamps, signals, nameboard and corrugated-iron platform store.

▷ In this early 20th-century view of Camerton station, the posing staff are rather upstaged by the line of wagons laden with the products of the Somerset coalfield. Milk churns indicate the more usual traffic on the branch – which in the 1950s became famous as the setting for the filming of *The Titfield Thunderbolt*.

▽ Pewsey is a rare survivor among rural Wiltshire stations. Here, in July 1975, a Class 50 diesel brings the Paddington-to-Paignton train into the platform while a small huddle of passengers – some quite possibly setting off for a Devon holiday – wait to board.

ALONG HOLIDAY LINES

The holiday resorts of the West Country owe more to the railways than to the weather, and much of their popularity dates back to the ever-expanding railway map of the Victorian era. The GWR and the LSWR were the major players in the holiday development of the region, the GWR being the first to call the Devon coast around Torquay the 'English Riviera'. By the late 1800s main lines and branch lines had opened up most of the Southwest to holiday traffic, and the railway companies were vital promoters of the beaches, towns and villages, rivers, woodland and moorland that might appeal to visitors. By the

20th century, famous named trains were the gateway for thousands of holidaymakers to this very extensive resort region, from Wiltshire to Cornwall.

∇ The first railways to reach Newquay, in the 1840s, were clay lines; passenger services did not start until some years later. From the early 1900s the GWR helped to turn Newquay into a fashionable resort. Here, on a rainy day at the end of their holiday in June 1980, passengers await the direct train to Paddington, to be hauled by the Class 47 diesel, No. 47097.

▷ On the cover of this 1954 edition of British Railways' famous series of annual holiday guides, a sophisticated young couple look out over a sweeping sandy beach. It could be the Mediterranean, but is probably Minehead or Torquay. These guides were widely used by holidaymakers seeking information about the region, its hotels and facilities, and how to get there.

▷ Camping coaches, launched in the mid-1930s, were immediately popular, and hundreds were in use all over Britain by the start of World War II. This photograph of a couple enjoying their tea, later re-issued as a cigarette card, was published by the GWR to promote camping coach holidays in remote parts of its network. The weekly cost for a party of six varied from £3 to £5.

◁ ▽ ▷ Holiday and excursion handbills and brochures show how extensively the railways promoted the West Country resorts from the 1920s to the 1980s, with many trains running directly from the Midlands and the North. Postcards, as ever, reflect the popularity of the region.

CAMPING COACH

SUMMER SATURDAY

West Country Trains

Compulsory Seat Reservations

Fast trains to get you from London and Reading to South West Holiday Resorts and back in reserved seat comfort on busy Summer Saturdays

Saturdays 28 May to 17 September 1983

London Paddington · Reading · Taunton · Barnstaple · Exeter · Dawlish · Exmouth · Teignmouth · Newton Abbot · Torquay · Totnes · Paignton · Plymouth · Liskeard · Gunnislake · Bodmin Road · Looe · Lostwithiel · Par · Newquay · St Austell · Truro · Redruth · Falmouth · Camborne · Hayle · St Ives · St Erth · Penzance

TRAVEL TO

Plymouth
The Holiday centre for Devon & Cornwall

All-in holidays in the WEST COUNTRY

ILFRACOMBE · WESTON-SUPER-MARE · MINEHEAD · TORQUAY · PAIGNTON

BY SPECIAL TRAIN FROM
NEWCASTLE DARLINGTON LEEDS SHEFFIELD

AND BY CONNECTING SERVICES FROM
SOUTH SHIELDS SUNDERLAND TYNEMOUTH
WHITLEY BAY MIDDLESBROUGH REDCAR
SALTBURN HARROGATE YORK

EVERY SATURDAY
25th MAY to 7th SEPTEMBER, 1963

ALL-IN PRICE INCLUDES :—
Travel Tickets · Reserved Seats on Trains
Meals on Trains · Hotel Accommodation
Sightseeing Trips · Gratuities

ORGANISED BY THE CREATIVE TOURIST AGENTS CONFERENCE
IN CONJUNCTION WITH BRITISH RAILWAYS

BRITISH RAILWAYS

B 393

L M S
LONDON MIDLAND AND SCOTTISH RAILWAY

SPRING AND EARLY SUMMER HOLIDAYS
IN THE WEST

On FRIDAY, APRIL 29th, and
EVERY FRIDAY until JULY 8th, inclusive
(except June 3rd)

COOK'S
PERIOD EXCURSIONS TO

Bath, Ilfracombe, Mortehoe
BUDLEIGH SALTERTON
EXETER, EXMOUTH
DEVONPORT, PLYMOUTH, Etc.
AND THE

WEST OF ENGLAND
(VIA BATH, TEMPLECOMBE, AND SOUTHERN RAILWAY)

St. Michael's Mount.

GOODRINGTON · COCKINGTON
THURLOE HOTEL SANDS ROAD PAIGNTON
PAIGNTON SANDS · THE HARBOUR

▽ ▷ Railway companies issued postcards and guide
books to encourage holiday traffic, with the LNWR
and the GWR being early pioneers in this field. Also
perennially popular was the Holiday Runabout ticket.
Publicity was frequently arranged jointly by the railway
and the local tourist board, as seen in the 1962 British
Railways brochure promoting Weston-super-Mare.

THE ESPLANADE LOOKING E.
SIDMOUTH

BOURNEMOUTH—INVALIDS WALK
THROUGH CARRIAGES TO & FROM THE L. & N.W. RAILWAY VIA WILLESDEN JUNCTION.

Great Western Railway.

THIRD CLASS
Holiday Season Ticket

No. 322   (1 Week)
                           Rate 10/-
Mr. Smith   Rate 10/6 N

From   9th Sept   to

1 5 SEP 1938

(YATTON)

Available between the Stations shown
the other side by the routes indicated.

GLORIOUS

DEVON

S.P.B.MAIS

British Rail
holiday
runabout
tickets

7 DAYS' UNLIMITED TRAVEL
THE WEST COUNTRY
DORSET · SOMERSET · DEVON · CORNWALL
THE COTSWOLDS · THE MALVERN HILLS
17 APRIL TO 29 OCTOBER 1966

WESTON
SUPER-MARE

..in Sunny Somerset

▽ The train journey was often the start of the holiday, an idea encouraged by a wide range of route guides, such as this Torbay Express example from the 1950s. The photograph, probably taken in the early 1960s, shows a Paddington-bound West Country express on the approach to Bath, while a couple in a rowing boat make the most of a sunny day on the river Avon.

THE *Torbay* EXPRESS

FEATURES OF INTEREST EN ROUTE

ALONG PRESERVED LINES

Britain's preserved railway movement, started by enthusiasts in the 1950s, is now a major part of the national heritage industry. There are lines all over the country, most of which still rely on the appeal of steam to attract enthusiasts, volunteers and visitors. Many operate regular timetabled services, but increasingly important are special events and themed days, several of which are featured on a regional basis. The West Somerset Railway, which operates over the former GWR branch to Minehead, is famous among other things for its Spring and Autumn Steam Galas, featuring visiting locomotives.

▽ Opened in 1874, the Minehead branch was built to bring a new generation of visitors to the town, and its status as a popular resort really dates from that point. Today the West Somerset Railway, a vital part of the local economy, still fulfils that aim. Here, on a fine day, visiting crowds spill out onto the platforms, many heading for the town after their 20-mile journey from Bishops Lydeard.

West Somerset Railway
SPRING STEAM GALA

Up to 5 Standard class locos!

92203

'GWR 175'
THE STANDARD ERA
20, 21 & 25-28 MARCH 2010

West Somerset Railway
Tel: 01643-704996   www.west-somerset-railway.co.uk

Spring Steam Gala One Day Rover Ticket

Sat 27 Mar 2010 8.00am
One Day of pure steam
A great day out for all the family
Unreserved Seating   £22.00

EXTRAS - No.11

Mr Paul Atterbury ATTE021674.ML00001849

◁ Steam galas bring out the crowds, many of whom come specially to see the visiting locomotives, often major names from other heritage railways. Here, one of the West Somerset's home team, GWR Class 4575 No. 5553, flanks a visiting A4 Pacific.

▽ A very famous visitor, LMS Royal Scot Class No. 6100, 'Royal Scot', tries out Minehead's new turntable. Brought in bits from Pwllheli in 1979, the turntable was restored to service in 2008 and has attracted many visitors to the railway.

▽ Double-heading is often a feature of a steam gala, sometimes with interesting locomotive pairings. Here a West Country class Bulleid Pacific from British Railways' Southern Region shares a heavy train with a BR Standard.

▽ Attracting the visitors at Minehead on Steam Gala Day is another famous LMS locomotive, a fine Stanier Class 5MT No. 45440. In fact, this is another Black Five, No. 45407, 'The Lancashire Fusilier', disguised as 45440, a noted locomotive from the old Somerset & Dorset route.

IN & AROUND THE STATION

There is a vast and largely unregarded archive of photographs of railwaymen and women at work in station settings. Dating back to the 1850s, and taken both formally and informally, these give us a remarkable insight into railway life and history, and underline the continual process of social change. They range from carefully posed groups to more individual and even casual shots, but they all show the sense of pride – in the job and the uniform – that once was shared by those who worked on the railway and was indicative of their position and status in society. These photographs offer a very accessible insight into a world that has changed beyond recognition.

➤ *Railway life in the past was all-encompassing, and the boundaries between professional and social life were vague. Brass bands were a common example of this, many being linked to railway works or major stations.*

↡ *A fairly informal photograph shows a group of Great Central Railway staff on an unidentified station. The presence of a woman in uniform, comfortably placed within the group, dates the occasion to World War I.*

▲ *On a wet day in 1897 the staff of Forest Hill station, part of the LB&SCR's south London suburban network, are formally grouped around Mr Scott, the stationmaster, resplendent in his top hat and his badge of office. The social and professional hierarchies are clear; even the dog knows his place.*

This group are posing on a Taff Vale Railway station in South Wales, probably in about 1905. They all look young, especially the boy on the right in the ill-fitting jacket and oversized collar. He may be a 'booking boy', responsible for keeping the train register in the signal box.

A jolly group, complete with ladies, soldiers and policemen, pose in the 1940s on the platform at Pontefract Baghill, Yorkshire, a station built by the Swinton & Knottingley Joint Railway during the 1870s.

Bridport station, near the end of a rural branch line in west Dorset, had opened in 1857 as a broad gauge line. The early photograph below shows the station staff posing beside one of the characteristic saddle tanks.

LONDON & NORTH EASTERN RAILWAY,
(NORTH EASTERN AREA.)

THIRD CLASS FREE PASS,

No. 22072

Mr

Between

From   19
To   19

George Davidson
Divisional General Manager

🚂 Tydd was a Lincolnshire station on the line from Wisbech to Sutton Bridge. On a quiet, sunny day in the Edwardian era, the station staff and the stationmaster's family have been brought together for an informal photograph.

🚂 Drumburgh was the junction for the short branch to Port Carlisle in Cumbria, a line operated for years by horse traction. Here, perhaps in the 1920s, the train waits while its crew pose with the station staff beneath the station nameboard.

🚂 A number of lines spread southwards from Ayr along the Doon valley in the 1850s, including a long branch to Dalmellington. This photograph shows the station staff, probably in the 1930s. It is an informal pose, but the hierarchy is evident.

🚂 This Great Eastern Railway group are making the most of their job as a station-cleaning gang. Someone, presumably one of the group, has written on the back of this early 20th-century postcard 'How would you like these to do your spring cleaning?' and then, in brackets, 'Some of the nuts'.

↞ Many railway stations prided themselves on their gardens, and national and local competitions were held to select the best examples. This is Wolferton station, in Norfolk. It was famous in the 1950s for its well-kept gardens and platform decorations, not least because it was used by the royal family on visits to Sandringham. Gardening might not have been part of normal office routine, but these ladies seem happy to help.

◗ A smiling group at Wolferton celebrates another award in the national Best Kept Station competition, at some point during the 1950s.

↞ Another view of some of the same staff at Wolferton, this time with the addition of the dog, who clearly wants nothing to do with the camera.

◗ The caption says this is a platelayers' cabin at Heckmondwike junction, West Yorkshire, but the photograph is really about the station garden and the men responsible for it.

PLATELAYERS CABIN

→ In this early 20th-century picture, a South Eastern & Chatham Railway stationmaster poses proudly for the photographer.

→ While there are numerous photographs of groups, there are also plenty of images of individual railwaymen. This informal portrait shows a restaurant car steward, probably snapped by a colleague as he was coming on or off duty, sometime during the 1920s.

← Apparently dating from the 1870s, this early carte de visite taken by a photographer in Tempsford, Bedfordshire, shows a Great Northern Railway signalman or pointsman posing on the station platform.

→ A member of the station staff poses informally on the platform at Potter Heigham, in Norfolk, during the late 1950s. Although he might be the only person on duty, he is looking relaxed and does not seem bothered that the photographer is obviously breaking the rules by standing on the track.

Modern images can be just as interesting as older ones. This photograph of a British Rail employee was taken at London's Waterloo station as recently as 1981 but, because it shows the new-style uniform introduced throughout the network from the 1970s, it already has a period quality.

In a more unusual pose, a railwayman at Upper Greenock stands slightly awkwardly on a painted tyre that appears to represent a minimal attempt at station gardening. This is during the 1970s, and the 1950s-style totem nameplates are still in place.

This 1972 photograph shows the ticket office at Newton Abbot station, in Devon. At this time, things were changing rapidly, and the old Edmundson card tickets were disappearing. However, there are plenty of reminders of the past, not least the furniture, the date stamps, the bowls for change and the piles of paperwork.

➤ In August 1961 at Grangemouth, on the Firth of Forth, the DMU is ready to depart. However, there is still time for a friendly photograph. The driver holds the single-line token.

➤ While the guard is technically in control of the train, he will wait for the all-clear from the dispatcher on the platform before he allows his train, in this case a London-bound express, to depart. This is Warrington Bank Quay in 1974.

START SMART...

STAY SMART

Supervisors
Employed at Passenger Stations

➤ From the 1960s British Rail became much more image-conscious, and a new look was introduced for its signage, publicity material and uniforms, the latter being designed to give a contemporary look. This version, for supervisors, dates from 1987.

7P5FA

34102

BRITISH RAILWAYS (E)   (F.1613)
FREE PASS & PRIVILEGE TICKET
OUTWARD AND RETURN
REGULATION TICKET
MR. ....
Issued by Traffic Manager, Sheffield

This delightfully informal photograph shows three Pullman car staff posing on the platform before going on duty on their train in the 1950s.

It is in the last months of steam on British Railways Southern Region, and in March 1967 West Country Class No. 34102, 'Lapford', waits to depart from London Bridge station. Driver Finish and Fireman Fox pass the time of day while Guard Crawforth finishes off his sandwich.

The maintenance of buildings and structures was usually the responsibility of dedicated teams. This scene shows a painter, probably a volunteer, hard at work on the Mid Hants Railway in the early days of preservation.

DRIVING THE TRAINS

To some, driving a train seemed the most romantic of jobs, yet throughout the age of steam a driver's job was dangerous, physically demanding, uncomfortable, not very well paid, and entailed working long hours with full responsibility for the locomotive and its train. Until the 1870s many locomotives had cabs open to the weather and, until the 1930s, few had seats. Despite all this, drivers and their firemen – who were in effect trainee drivers – enjoyed the status that came with this highly structured job and were regarded as reliable, trustworthy men. The coming of diesels, with comfortable seats in enclosed cabs and much easier controls, greatly improved the driver's life, and soon led to single manning and woman drivers.

↦ *Even on a large mainline express locomotive, the cab was a restricted space with bits of metal everywhere that were either hot or sharp, or both. Forward visibility was limited and, when travelling at speed, it was often difficult to stand without having to hold on to something. Driver and fireman worked continuously as a team, keeping out of each other's way and sharing the responsibility for watching the controls and the track and signals ahead.*

With a well-defined pattern of shift operation, crews changed at set locations. Four men on the footplate, as seen in the photograph on the opposite page, was, therefore, a rare sight. In order to run its London-to-Edinburgh non-stop service, the LNER needed two crews. The relief crew travelled on the train until changeover time, when they made their way onto the footplate via a specially built tender with a narrow corridor along one side. Here, the second crew emerges from the corridor tender to take over control of the moving locomotive on the footplate.

Traditionally, trains in Britain have always run on the left, while steam locomotives have been driven from the right-hand side of the cab. The LNER's Shire Class engines were, unusually, left-hand drive, as shown in this photograph. It is a powerful and carefully posed image, but actually nothing is happening. There is no fire, no dust on the floor and no pressure on the gauge.

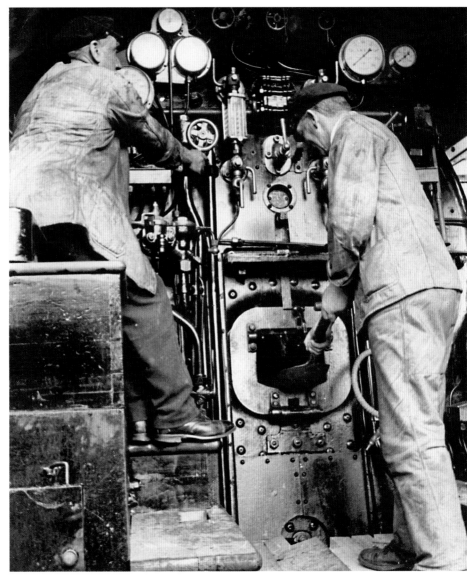

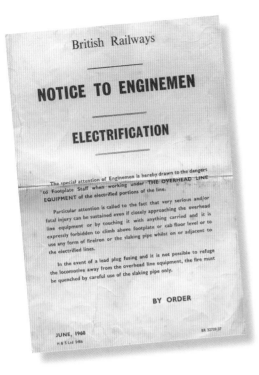

British Railways

NOTICE TO ENGINEMEN

ELECTRIFICATION

The special attention of Enginemen is hereby drawn to the dangers to Footplate Staff when working under THE OVERHEAD LINE EQUIPMENT of the electrified portions of the line.

Particular attention is called to the fact that very serious and/or fatal injury can be sustained even if closely approaching the overhead line equipment or by touching it with anything carried and it is expressly forbidden to climb above footplate or cab floor level or to use any form of fireiron or the slaking pipe whilst on or adjacent to the electrified lines.

In the event of a lead plug fusing and it is not possible to refuge the locomotive away from the overhead line equipment, the fire must be quenched by careful use of the slaking pipe only.

BY ORDER

JUNE, 1960

BR 32709/37

H & S Ltd 5486

There are many photographs of drivers and firemen posing on the footplate, most of which were taken in the shed or in other places where the locomotive was out of use or not in steam. Action shots of locomotives actually being driven are less common, partly because the photographer usually stood on top of the tender, a highly dangerous place at speed. This LNWR crew was photographed at Northampton shed.

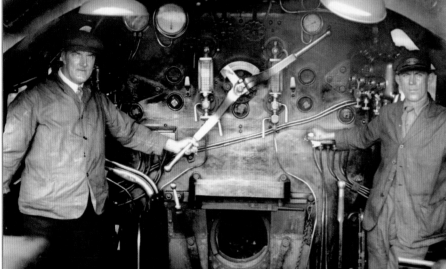

Driver Hudson and Fireman Cummins pose on the footplate of a locomotive on display at an exhibition at Hounslow. The locomotive is in steam but is probably only moving up and down an exhibition track, allowing the crew ample time for the photographer.

Another carefully posed driving shot from the 1920s or 1930s, perhaps for one of the many articles on train driving that were published in popular magazines. The driver, hand firmly on the regulator, leans out of the cab for a view of the signals ahead.

⬆ While the fireman keeps a lookout, the driver eases his elderly locomotive during track lifting in 1963 at Withington, in Gloucestershire, following the closure of the Midland & South Western Junction Railway line. It is from a class of GWR 2-8-0 freight locomotives introduced in 1903. The photographer is standing in a derelict signal box, dating back to the days of the M&SWJR.

▶ This is a typical enthusiast's photograph from the late 1950s or early 1960s, showing the driver, fireman and guard resting between duties on an ex-NER Class J25 locomotive. It is in Northeast England, but the exact location was not recorded.

(PRIVATE and not for publication)   SECTION E

BRITISH RAILWAYS

EASTERN REGION

WORKING TIMETABLE

OF

MANDATORY TRAIN SERVICES

BETWEEN

CHESTERFIELD & LEEDS TO SELBY, YORK
AND SCARBOROUGH

SHEFFIELD TO LEEDS & BRADFORD EXCHANGE
VIA BARNSLEY & NORMANTON

LEEDS TO YORK (VIA HARROGATE) AND SKIPTON
& BRANCHES

7 MAY 1973 to 5 MAY 1974

When trains are running late, drivers must endeavour to make up time,
with due regard to all speed restrictions and the braking capability
of the train

F. J. BURGE
CHIEF OPERATING MANAGER

Issued at
YORK

PRINTED BY ALBERT GAIT LTD., BARNSLEY

◗ *This is Cambridge in 1955,
and there is a bit of time
for the driver and fireman to
enjoy a cigarette while their
charge, Britannia Class No.
70002, 'Geoffrey Chaucer',
takes on water.*

70002

🔺 By the 1970s overalls and traditional grease top caps were a thing of the past, as drivers, comfortable in their cabs, took on the new-look British Rail corporate uniform. However, for this former steam driver old habits die hard and he has kept on his old overall jacket under the new corporate overcoat.

🔺 The advent of diesels greatly improved the working conditions for drivers and gradually put firemen out of a job. Yet steam habits, and steam uniforms, lingered on, along with the practice of posing beside the locomotive. In the 1960s, three drivers, Messrs Shorten, Kirman and Blyth, stand in front of a new-looking Class 31 diesel. This locomotive has since been preserved.

🔺 This 1970s photograph illustrates both the comfort of the driving position in a modern electric or diesel locomotive and, thanks to the sophisticated engineering and electronics, the relative simplicity of the controls.

ASSOCIATED SOCIETY OF LOCOMOTIVE
ENGINEERS, FIREMEN, CLEANERS AND
MOTORMEN

MEMBER'S
CONTRIBUTION CARD

HEAD OFFICE :
9, ARKWRIGHT ROAD, HAMPSTEAD, LONDON, N.W.3

➤ On a sunny February day in 1962, a relief driver and fireman, seated on an old GWR bench at Gloucester Central station, watch an oil tank train passing through, headed by a stained and grimy BR Standard Class locomotive. Soon, their duty roster will start and it will be back to work.

➤ In the late Victorian and Edwardian eras, it was common practice to photograph locomotives when they were new or recently overhauled, often posed outside the shed. Sometimes the crew were included, usually in the cab but occasionally, as in this LSWR example, beside the locomotive. Clearly revealed here is the professional relationship between driver and fireman, with no doubt about who is in charge.

↟ Caught between duties by a photographer, a fireman, guard and driver take a rest on a bench on a warm day. They have been joined by an elderly local. His jacket suggests he might be a retired driver.

↟ Seated on the buffer beam of their LMS Patriot Class locomotive, No. 45525, 'Colwyn Bay', a driver and fireman pose for the photographer. They seem relaxed, as though their duties have yet to begin. The locomotive was based at Edge Hill, Liverpool, probably in the late 1950s.

↝ Driving to and fro along the Hayling Island branch line from Havant, Hampshire, cannot have been the most demanding or exciting of duties, particularly in the 1960s with closure imminent. There is some time to go before the next departure and there are still no passengers, so it is a good moment to rest on a platform bench while the Class A1X Terrier tank engine, No. 32678, quietly simmers away.

↟ An old locomotive and an elderly driver, grease can in hand, stand together for a photographer in the LMS region during the 1920s.

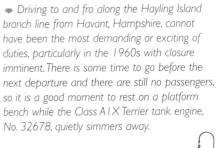

GUARDS ON DUTY

Descended from the men employed to guard the mail, the railway guard emerged in the 1840s, with clear and ever-increasing responsibilities for the efficient and safe operation of the train. Passenger guards soon became important and well-dressed figures, responsible for mail, parcels, luggage, animals and children travelling alone, as well as the safety of all passengers and the train. The goods guard had a harder life, working alone in the brake van at the rear, in charge of braking the train.

➤ The Padarn Railway, a 4ft gauge line linking slate quarries at Dinorwic with the harbour at Port Dinorwic, North Wales, was opened in 1843 and closed in 1961. Here, in July 1950, the guard applies the brake to control the speed of the train, while keeping an eye on his rake of 'host' wagons, each carrying four loaded narrow gauge slate trucks. Guarding this train over the 6-mile route would not have been too arduous.

➤ In 1950 there were nearly 20,000 goods guards but only 8,000 passenger guards. Until continuous braking became universal from the 1970s, every goods train had a brake van. Here the guard spent many solitary hours, comforted only by a stove and responsible for controlling the train's braking – a very skilled activity.

In 1936 on the Sheppey Light Railway in Kent, the guard checks his solitary passenger, a young boy, probably left in his care. As so often, a remote branch line has become a haven for elderly carriages. This example began life as part of an articulated railcar set before World War I.

Guard and stationmaster share a joke and pose for the camera on the platform at Alton station in Hampshire, probably in the 1950s. Smart uniforms and floral buttonholes were something they had in common, reflecting their status and their place in the public eye.

At Ogmore Vale, a station on the Nantymoel branch in South Wales, the guard, flag in hand, walks back alongside his train to speed its departure. Time-keeping was one of the guard's many responsibilities.

The guard gives the 'right away' to the prototype HST 125 after a brief stop at Stapleton Road, Bristol, on a trial run from Bristol to Paddington in June 1975.

When paytrains were introduced in the 1960s as part of a programme to reduce staffing levels, the role of the guards changed considerably and they became conductors.

PAYTRAIN is coming to your local station

SERVICE STARTS 15 JUNE 1969

Eastern Paytrain

STUDIO PORTRAITS

By the late 1850s many towns in Britain had at least one photographer's studio. Universally popular was the small *carte de visite*, a form of photograph developed in France from 1854, and these were widely used to record working men in uniform. By the early 1900s photographs could be printed in postcard format, and this, along with the availability of simple portable cameras, led to a decline in the popularity of the studio portrait. However, the legacy is a remarkable archive of images of anonymous 19th-century railwaymen, from porters to stationmasters, whose pride in their job, and their uniform, is obvious.

◆ The studio props and the style of uniform suggest that this picture of a Great Northern Railway employee dates from about the 1860s. The uniform is battered, but still worn with pride.

▲ This rather formal portrait of a Great Western Railway guard could perhaps have been taken to celebrate a rise in seniority.

◆ Unusually, this Great Eastern Railway stationmaster chose to be photographed in the studio with his wife. It is in the Edwardian era and they were perhaps celebrating a new appointment, or even their recent marriage.

◆ It was not unusual for railway staff to remain in employment well past their sixties, particularly in rural areas, but this Victorian guard must surely have been approaching retirement when he visited the photographer.

◗ This man took his sons to the studio. It is not known which railway he was working for, but the date is about 1910. Perhaps the boy on the right is following in his footsteps.

◆ This Midland Railway employee was probably photographed in the 1870s or 1880s. The pose is formal, but relaxed.

◆ Another Midland Railway photograph, but this one shows a stationmaster, with watch chain and suitably imposing presence, in about 1900.

◆ The badges worn by this young man, perhaps a porter, suggest he worked jointly for both the Midland Railway and the North Eastern Railway at some shared station.

◗ This late Victorian South Eastern Railway porter's pride is apparent. He has done his best to look smart for the photographer, even though his uniform has seen better days.

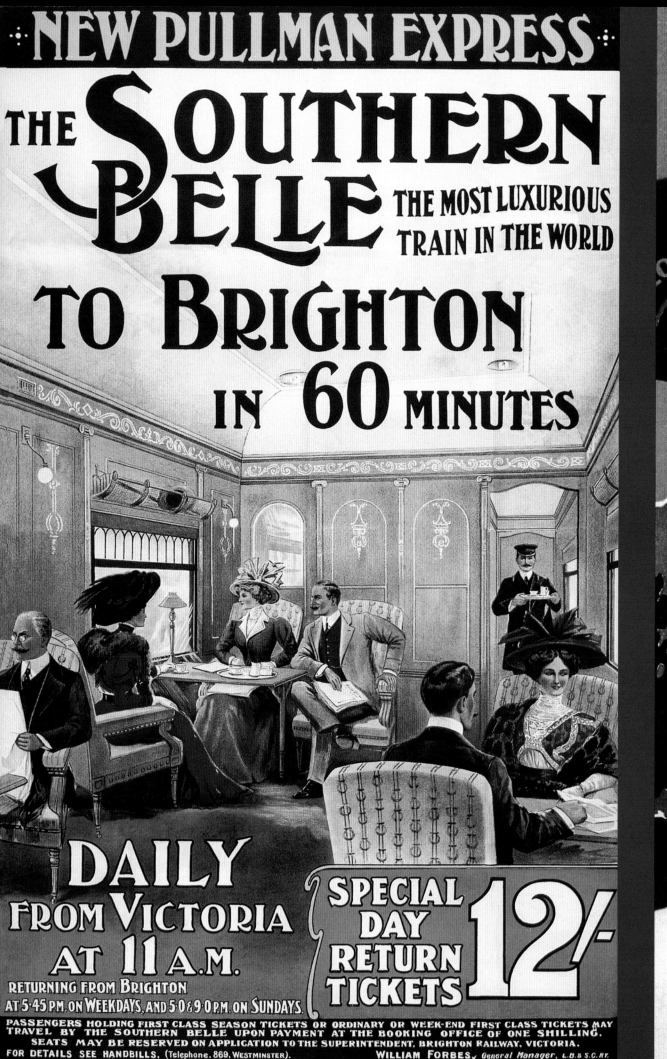

IN AND AROUND SOUTHERN ENGLAND

ALLHALLOWS-ON-SEA

WESTCLIFF

ALLHALLOWS

SOUTHERN RAILWAY

GRAVESEND

CHATHAM

MAIDSTONE

R.BURLEY

LTHY HOMES
LONDONERS
37 MILES FROM THE CITY
VER 2 MILES FIRM GOLDEN SANDS

STATION SCENES

Southern England is one of the densest parts of the national railway map, criss-crossed with lines built primarily for commuter traffic. When the network was at its peak, there were also a number of main lines serving coastal resorts and harbours, along with a rich variety of rural routes and branch lines, many now lost. London sits at the region's heart, the routes radiating from its many termini. Dating back to the 1830s, these great stations, constantly enlarged and rebuilt, document through photographs the growth of railway traffic during the Victorian period. At the same time, other images and postcards indicate the changing patterns of railway travel – and reveal some of the forgotten corners.

▽ Until its rebuilding in the early 1990s, London Liverpool Street was a vast station with a confusion of platforms linked by an overhead walkway. Here, in the 1920s, holiday crowds pack the concourse.

▷ This Edwardian card shows passengers using Liverpool Street's original entrance, part of the 1875 station planned by Edward Wilson in French Gothic style. The station was expanded in 1894.

EXTERIOR OF LIVERPOOL STREET STATION, LONDON.

△ Until 1924 London Victoria was two adjacent stations built by rival companies, and its grandiose architecture underlines that rivalry. This late 1930s, or possibly 1940s, view shows the eastern part, as rebuilt in 1908 for the London, Brighton & South Coast Railway. The Grosvenor Hotel of 1864 is to the right of the wonderfully uncluttered bus station.

△ This 1905 card, extravagantly overwritten by a Frenchman to his friend in Strasbourg, shows the original LB&SCR terminus, little more than a massive trainshed faced by a series of sheds and a porte cochère. This muddle, and the grand structure being created next door by the SECR, was the impetus for the 1908 rebuilding.

◁ Euston, opened from 1837, was London's first mainline terminus and its most famous feature was Hardwick's great Doric arch, or propylaeum. To the nation's horror, this was destroyed in 1961, along with most of the original station. This card, posted in July 1908, gives a sense of what was lost by this act of vandalism.

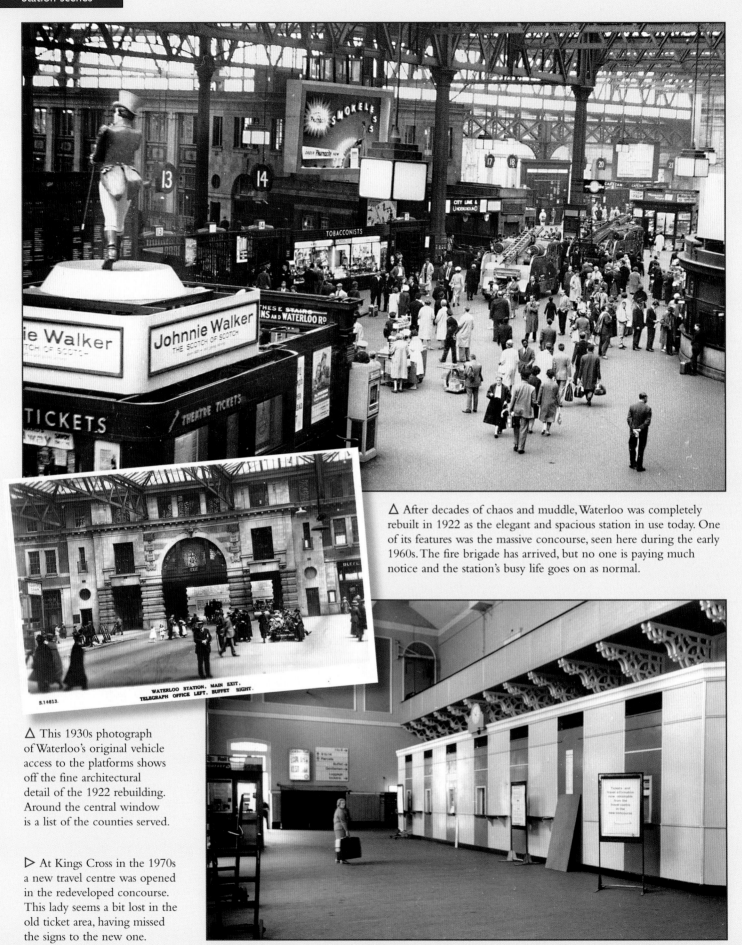

△ After decades of chaos and muddle, Waterloo was completely rebuilt in 1922 as the elegant and spacious station in use today. One of its features was the massive concourse, seen here during the early 1960s. The fire brigade has arrived, but no one is paying much notice and the station's busy life goes on as normal.

△ This 1930s photograph of Waterloo's original vehicle access to the platforms shows off the fine architectural detail of the 1922 rebuilding. Around the central window is a list of the counties served.

▷ At Kings Cross in the 1970s a new travel centre was opened in the redeveloped concourse. This lady seems a bit lost in the old ticket area, having missed the signs to the new one.

◁ BR's public relations people were responsible for this evocative 1960 view of the ticket hall at Gunnersbury station. With the plethora of notices and an apparently abandoned bicycle, it is a scene full of period charm.

◁ Equally evocative is this picture of a quiet corner at Kings Cross, just before Christmas in 1958. There are piles of mail and luggage, but the station is almost deserted. Opened in 1852, the terminus was famous for its powerfully simple style.

△ The Southern Railway was famous for its extensive network of electric suburban services and the third rail that powered them. This is Norbiton station, in Surrey, in the summer of 1955, and a British Railways green 4-SUB non-corridor electric train waits in the platform. The driver leans against his train, watching a family sorting themselves out before either leaving the station or getting on the train. It is a leisurely scene.

△ This card shows a busy scene at Uckfield station in the Edwardian era. The platform is crowded with passengers awaiting the arriving train, and a porter is wheeling along a well-laden trolley. Now Uckfield is the end of the line; then it was on a popular route linking Tunbridge Wells and Brighton via Lewes.

◁ Wandsworth Common is a typical commuter station served by trains from Victoria. Today it is not remarkable, but in the early 1900s it was quite substantial – and boasted large, regimented flower beds. It must have been a quiet day when the photographer of this card visited, and everyone had time to pose.

S 7222   L. B. & S. C. RAILWAY STATION, WANDSWORTH COMMON, LONDON

▷ The Isle of Wight's eccentric and idiosyncratic railway network was much loved, representing as it did the survival of a Victorian railway into the middle of the 20th century. This is Brading in the 1960s, shortly before the closure of most of the system. The station has seen better, and busier, days but services are still running and enthusiasts are keen to document the scene. The photographer has gone into forbidden territory beyond the platform to capture the scene while his friend notes the locomotive's number. Meanwhile a passenger, or perhaps another spotter, runs across the footbridge.

▽ This is Wroxhall, on the Isle of Wight, in September 1965. The train from Ryde to Ventnor drifts into the platform as the driver leans out to hand over the single-line token. Passengers, including a young mother who perhaps is introducing her child to the delights of trainspotting, watch from the opposite platform.

CRAWLEY & HORSHAM POINT-TO-POINT RACES
SATURDAY 14 APRIL AT PARHAM·STORRINGTON·FIRST RACE 2.30 TOTALISATOR

CAFETERIA

EVENING ARGUS

W.H.SMITH&SON

TRAIN ARRIVALS

△ Brighton has a classic seaside terminus station, set high above the town and still recognizably the building designed by David Mocatta and opened in 1841 by the London & Brighton Railway. In this 1950s view, the station concourse buzzes with everyday station life.

▽ Victorian railway companies were keen promoters of tourism, but many of their ambitious schemes came to nought. Typical was the short branch line serving Allhallows-on-Sea, on the north coast of the Isle of Grain. Allhallows never got going as a resort and few people used the railway, as this photograph shows. It closed in 1961.

△ The Canterbury & Whitstable Railway was one of the first
passenger-carrying lines in Britain, opening in 1830. This Edwardian
view shows the level crossing at the start of the branch serving the
harbour, originally opened in 1832 and closed in 1953. In a typically
posed scene, everyone is looking at the camera: a lady with a pram, a
young girl, and a gentleman doing his best to keep his balance on his
bicycle while the picture is taken.

▽ In the first decades of the 20th century many railway companies
experimented with railcars for use on little-used rural routes and branch
lines. This 1920s photograph shows a petrol-engined and chain-driven
example built for the Southern Railway by the Drewry Car Company.
Seen here being tried out by senior company managers, it could
carry 25 passengers and had a compartment for milk churns.

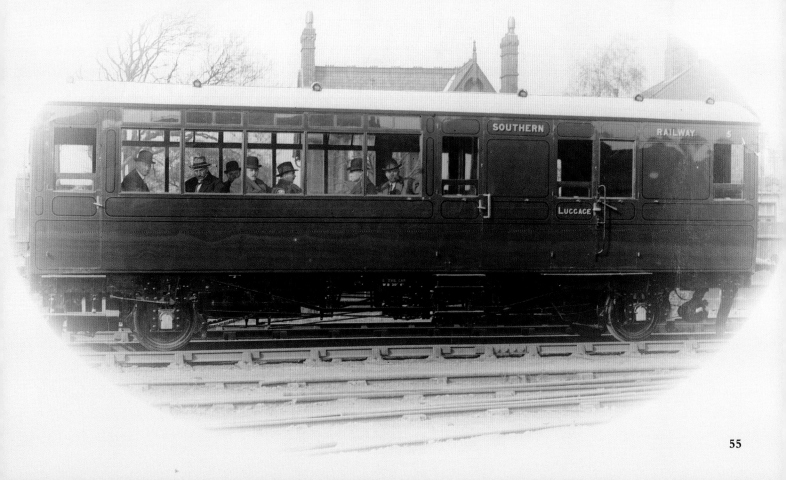

ALONG HOLIDAY LINES

Southern England still has a dense railway network, although many rural and cross-country lines have gone. Brighton, Portsmouth, Southampton and the Kent coast arrived early on the railway map of the South, and lines to these and other popular coastal destinations were soon carrying holiday traffic. Ramsgate, for example, received its first station in 1846, though the better-known Ramsgate Harbour station, right by the beach, did not open until 1863. Throughout the Victorian era resorts were added to the map of southern England. The Southern Railway and, later, British Railways, did their best to hold on to this important holiday traffic. London, at the heart of the network, was also an important holiday destination.

◁ ▽ The Isle of Wight was in effect a complete resort, thanks to its popularity with Queen Victoria, Lord Tennyson and others. Sealink, British Rail's shipping arm, operated car ferry services, although many holiday visitors relied on the island's railways. This scene on Cowes station was captured in July 1958.

▷ The Big Four railway companies, and subsequently British Railways, published annual holiday guides, with routes, descriptions of places of interest and lists of hotels.

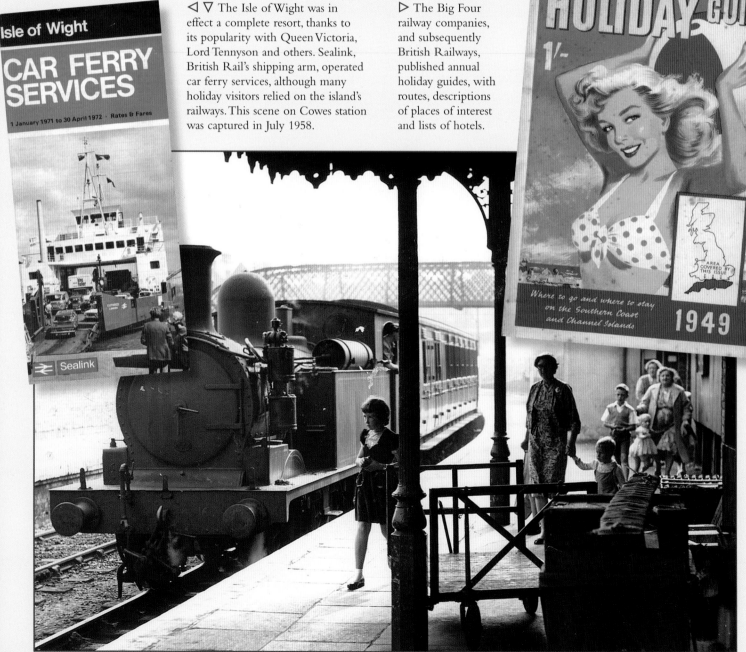

Isle of Wight
CAR FERRY SERVICES
1 January 1971 to 30 April 1972 · Rates & Fares

Sealink

SOUTHERN BRITISH RAILWAYS REGION
HOLIDAY GUIDE
1/-
Where to go and where to stay on the Southern Coast and Channel Islands
AREA COVERED BY THIS ISSUE
1949

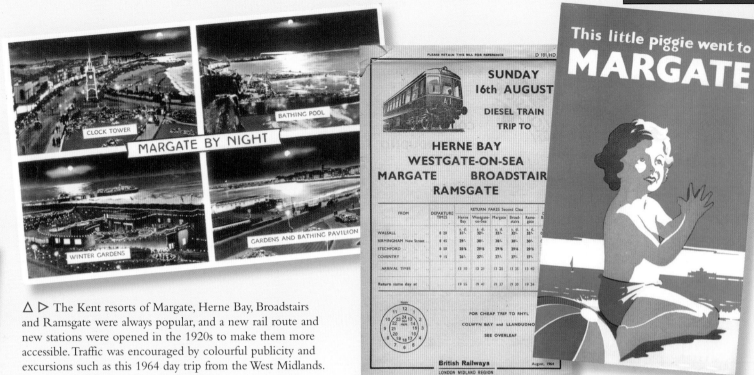

MARGATE BY NIGHT
CLOCK TOWER
BATHING POOL
WINTER GARDENS
GARDENS AND BATHING PAVILION

PLEASE RETAIN THIS BILL FOR REFERENCE   D 181/HD

SUNDAY
16th AUGUST

DIESEL TRAIN
TRIP TO

HERNE BAY
WESTGATE-ON-SEA
MARGATE   BROADSTAIRS
RAMSGATE

FROM	DEPARTURE TIMES	RETURN FARES Second Class				
		Herne Bay	Westgate-on-Sea	Margate	Broad-stairs	Rams-gate
		s. d.	s. d.	s. d.	s. d.	s. d.
WALSALL	8 20	31/-	32/-	32/-	32/-	32/-
BIRMINGHAM New Street	8 45	29/-	30/-	30/-	30/-	30/-
STECHFORD	8 50	29/6	29/6	29/6	29/6	29/6
COVENTRY	9 15	26/-	27/-	27/-	27/-	27/-
ARRIVAL TIMES		13 10	13 21	13 25	13 35	13 40
Return same day at		19 55	19 41	19 37	19 30	19 24

FOR CHEAP TRIP TO RHYL
COLWYN BAY and LLANDUDNO
SEE OVERLEAF

British Railways   August, 1964
LONDON MIDLAND REGION

This little piggie went to
MARGATE

△ ▷ The Kent resorts of Margate, Herne Bay, Broadstairs and Ramsgate were always popular, and a new rail route and new stations were opened in the 1920s to make them more accessible. Traffic was encouraged by colourful publicity and excursions such as this 1964 day trip from the West Midlands.

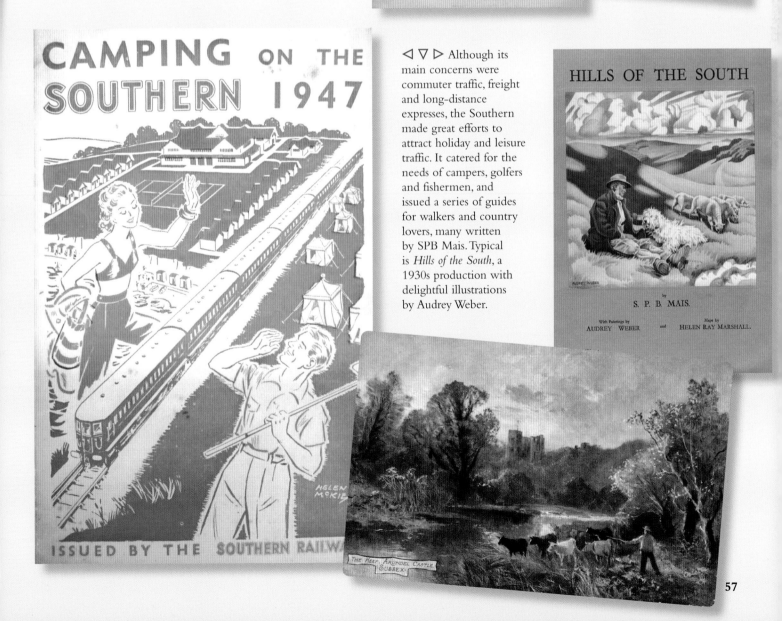

CAMPING ON THE SOUTHERN 1947

HELEN McKIE

ISSUED BY THE SOUTHERN RAILWAY

◁ ▽ ▷ Although its main concerns were commuter traffic, freight and long-distance expresses, the Southern made great efforts to attract holiday and leisure traffic. It catered for the needs of campers, golfers and fishermen, and issued a series of guides for walkers and country lovers, many written by SPB Mais. Typical is *Hills of the South*, a 1930s production with delightful illustrations by Audrey Weber.

HILLS OF THE SOUTH

AUDREY WEBER

by
S. P. B. MAIS.

With Paintings by
AUDREY WEBER   and   HELEN RAY MARSHALL.

THE KEEP, ARUNDEL CASTLE, SUSSEX.

CARLISLE PARADE - HASTINGS (LOOKING EAST)

SOUTHERN RAILWAY.
ISLE OF WIGHT HOLIDAY RUN-ABOUT TICKET
MONDAY TO FRIDAY INCLUSIVE.
No 451   THIRD CLASS
Available between Stations shewn on back hereof.
Expiring 2 1 AUG 1953

Signature of Holder E Smallbone
Rate £0. 10. 6

Conducted rambles
in the Southern Counties

July to December 1970

British Rail | Southern

7 day Runabout tickets

7 days 2nd class rail travel for £10

CHILDREN £5.00
5-15 years

1 April to 31 October 1982

Southern

◁ ▷ △ ▽ British Railways continued to cater for walkers into the 1960s. Also popular were Runabout tickets: the Isle of Wight ticket (above) is dated August 1953, when the island's entire network was still in use, while the Runabout leaflet from 1982 offered a choice of four areas. Postcards show how popular were resorts like Hastings, seen above in 1922. Below is a decorative vision of the Brighton train leaving London Bridge in 1908.

17 L·N·E·R

TOURIST
TRAVEL
FACILITIES

EXCURSIONS
DURING
SEPTEMBER

FROM
FENCHURCH STREET
KING'S CROSS
AND
LIVERPOOL STREET

For cheap facilities to race meetings, football matches and other sporting events,
see separate announcements

A. 291/300

MAY 1938

HALF DAY EXCURSIONS
FROM KING'S CROSS LIVERPOOL ST MARYLEBONE

LONDON & NORTH EASTERN RAILWAY

LONDON

from
KING'S CROSS
LIVERPOOL ST.
MARYLEBONE
and
Suburban Stations

LONDON & NORTH EASTERN RAILWAY

△ ◁ London was a significant destination in its own right, and railway companies such as the LMS and the LNER encouraged holiday travel to the capital. Also popular were excursions from London, as these British Railways handbills indicate.

ALONG PRESERVED LINES

The Bluebell Railway, a dedicated steam line and an important pioneer in the preservation movement, celebrated its 50th anniversary in 2010. Throughout its long history, the Bluebell has maintained a close historical and stylistic association with the Southern Railway and its predecessors. It operates as a branch line over part of the original through route, which ran from Lewes to East Grinstead (now the target for extension plans), and it is this branchline quality, along with its Victorian and classic locomotives and vehicles, that gives the railway a particular appeal. Special events include Toy & Rail Collectors' Fairs, Family Fun Weekends, and other familiar preserved line themes and activities.

△ An evocative night scene, at a special evening event for photographers, with a visitor from the Isle of Wight Steam Railway, the Terrier tank locomotive 'Freshwater'.

▽ The operation of period goods trains is always popular with visitors and photographers. This shows two SE&CR locomotives, one at the head of a classic mixed goods of the pre-World War I era.

▽ For volunteers, the appeal of a preserved railway is broad, and many particular skills are required for tasks ranging from station duties to locomotive maintenance. Here, one of the footplate crew poses in the cab of the railway's 1896 Stirling 01 Class locomotive.

▽ As is the case with main lines, track repair and maintenance is an important but little appreciated part of the safe and successful operation of a preserved line. Here, volunteers are working on the track on Freshfield Bank, a mile from Sheffield Park station.

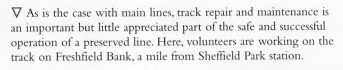

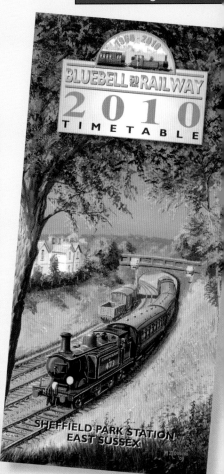

◁ Volunteers in the Carriage & Wagon Department apply the final varnish to one of the set of four Metropolitan Railway carriages, dating from the Edwardian era.

▷ All preserved lines have a backlog of locomotives and vehicles awaiting attention. Here, volunteers work on the gradual restoration of the frames from a locomotive tender to their original condition.

SIGNALLING

The history of railway signalling is a progression from handheld flags, bells and lamps to complete electronic systems. In between were mechanical semaphores, first used in the 1840s, interlocking, the block telegraph system and coloured lights – all advances driven by increased traffic and concerns for safety, often following serious accidents. The signal box, a familiar feature of the railway landscape, emerged from the 1860s and remained unchanged until the electronic age. Generations of signalmen, often leading lonely but demanding and highly responsible lives, are commemorated in photographs such as these.

◄ Signalmen in charge of small or isolated boxes often worked long duty shifts on their own. The large boxes at main city stations were a different matter, manned continuously by teams working together. This unusual photograph shows all the London & South Western Railway staff from the main box at Waterloo station, London, in about 1910. Included in the group are a young trainee and a man in charge of the fire pump.

➤ The box at The Mound on the Wick and Thurso line, north of Inverness, controlled traffic on the main line and the Dornoch branch. The great railway historian C Hamilton Ellis took this photograph of the LMS signalman at work, perhaps during the 1930s.

◗ This classic view shows the timber-built box at Plumpton in Sussex, complete with old block instruments, the line diagram and oil lamps. The photograph was taken during a visit by a retired signalman.

☛ Another view of Plumpton, showing a signalman making the most of a quiet moment and having a trim from a colleague. A signalman's life was often busy and there was plenty of paperwork to be kept up with. It was a profession that appealed to the self-contained and to those comfortable with their own company.

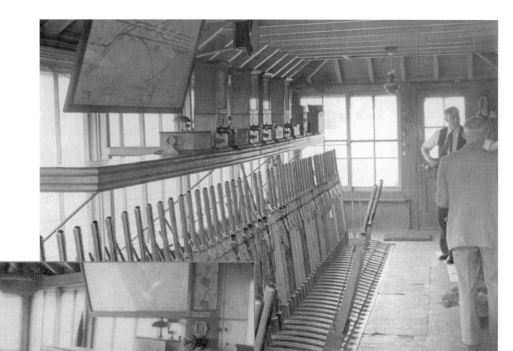

☛ One of the signalman's many duties was the control of the single-line tokens. Here, at Woodville, on the Swadlingcote loop in Derbyshire, the signalman exchanges tokens with a driver.

☚ This 1960s view shows the modern automated box at Chislehurst, in Kent, which controlled the complex junction shown on the diagram. Small switches have replaced the heavy levers, much improving the signalman's life.

⬆ Small boxes controlled level crossings and local sidings or goods yards. Some were built on the platform but others, like this example on British Railways Southern Region, stood alone. The man on duty here enjoys a pipe while watching the photographer – who is standing in the middle of the tracks.

⬆ This basic wooden box controlled a junction at Colehouse Lane, on the old Weston, Clevedon & Portishead Railway in Somerset. The signalman, neatly dressed, stands stiffly at attention for the photograph. Perhaps, like many railwaymen, he had formerly been a soldier.

⬇ Something out of the ordinary is happening at Western Junction box on the North London Railway. The driver has stopped his locomotive and is climbing down from the cab. Meanwhile, the signalman is greeting his important lady visitor as officials look on.

GREAT WESTERN RAILWAY

INSTRUCTIONS

For Signalling Trains during
FOGS and FALLING SNOW
and in Frosty Weather.

Private and not for Publication.

TO APPLY UNTIL FURTHER NOTICE

Signals were regularly maintained and checked, as so much depended on their safe operation. Here, in the 1930s, a team is hard at work on a mainline gantry near Hatfield, in Hertfordshire.

Apart from looking after the signals in his area, the signalman was also quite often in charge of the lamps. In the pre-electronic age, cleaning and refilling the lamps was a daily ritual to be carried out on every semaphore signal.

The manual exchange of single-line tokens, staffs or tablets was normal practice but, partly because of safety concerns with this process, machines were developed for mechanical exchange. Here, as a small boy watches, a signalman sets the mechanical tablet machine at Edmondthorpe & Wymondham, Leicestershire.

MAINTENANCE WORK

In many ways the most important, but least considered, part of any railway network is its infrastructure. Keeping buildings, structures and signalling up to date and in good repair is vital, and ongoing, work. Even more crucial is the maintenance of the track. Rails and their fittings must be regularly checked and replaced, along with sleepers and ballast. The network today requires 3 million tons of new ballast each year. In the 19th century and up to the 1940s most track repair and replacement was done by hand, necessitating the employment of large numbers of permanent way gangs. Since the 1960s the process has been increasingly mechanized and, with computers and lasers, maintenance now is probably better than ever.

◀ The GWR was an ambitious publisher with a substantial book list, including Track Topics, issued in 1935. This book of railway engineering was aimed at 'boys of all ages' and covered everything except locomotives and rolling stock.

▲ In 1962 a London-bound express passes Clink Road Junction near Frome, in Somerset, headed by 'Superb', a Type 4 Warship Class diesel. A permanent way gang, standing well back, salute the driver.

Platelayers, or gangers, pause from their continuous job of resetting the track and replacing the ballast to pose for the camera. This essential and labour-intensive work went on 24 hours a day, particularly on main lines. Today, machines do much of the work.

Railways were dangerous places, especially for those working on the track, and many companies issued safety manuals to make their employees aware of the risks and to give clear instructions about the correct way of doing things. This is a GWR version, first issued in 1936.

LOOK OUT!

Traditionally, all over Britain, local permanent way gangs were responsible for short sections of track. As a result there were thousands of lineside huts, in timber, brick or concrete, used as shelters and tool stores. Many survive, generally derelict and overgrown. In 1965 these gangers are not even bothering to watch this rare steam special.

This photograph shows a gang of men building up the embankment that leads to the famous Petherick Bridge on the Padstow branch in north Cornwall, probably when the line was being built. It opened in 1899. The amount of maintenance required in the future would, as ever, relate directly to the care taken over the initial construction work.

Complicated components such as a set of points were usually prefabricated and brought to the site ready for installation. This 1930s photograph shows the engineering involved.

◀ In the summer of 1969 a permanent way gang, now wearing reflective jackets, pose for the camera by Shap Summit signal box. Also posing, though probably not stopping, is a relatively new Class 50 locomotive, D417, 'Royal Oak', at the head of a container train.

SHAP SUMMIT

Track laying by night *(From a poster by Terence Cuneo)*

PERMANENT WAY
MECHANISED EQUIPMENT

BRITISH RAILWAYS   OCTOBER 1951

◆ When British Railways issued this booklet in 1954, with its dramatic cover by Terence Cuneo, mechanization of permanent way work was in its infancy, though cranes had always been used.

◆ This cheerful-looking permanent way gang, photographed somewhere in Southwest England in the 1920s, are ready for their day's work. Many are wearing the characteristic 'uniform' of waistcoat, collarless shirt and flat cap.

Electrification started early in the 20th century in northern England. In the 1930s Southern Railway began using the third-rail system to electrify much of its suburban network, as celebrated by this 1935 timetable booklet. Overhead electrification expanded greatly from the 1950s, with over 3,000 miles complete by 1994. This photograph shows work on the Braintree line in 1977.

SOUTHERN ELECTRIC

TIME TABLES OF NEW SERVICES SEASON & CHEAP TICKETS FARES

LONDON- SEAFORD- EASTBOURNE- BEXHILL- St LEONARDS AND HASTINGS

JULY 7th 1935, AND UNTIL FURTHER NOTICE.

PREVENTION OF ACCIDENTS

TO MEN WORKING ON OR ABOUT THE PERMANENT WAY

These men are maintaining the water troughs somewhere on the LNER network in 1927. At this time, troughs were commonplace on main lines, to allow locomotives to refill their water tenders using a scoop system, without stopping. This image gives a wonderful sense of the length of the trough.

The gangers' trolley was a familiar sight all over the network, used to transport men and materials to the workplace. For decades they were hand-operated, but motorized versions appeared after World War I. This example is passing Llandinam station, near Llanidloes in Central Wales.

◀ Everything requires a maintenance schedule, including the station lighting. This early 20th-century view shows the platform gas lighting being cleaned and repaired at Preston, Lancashire, probably on a quiet Sunday morning.

▶ The caption of this 1930s photograph says it all: 'A lofty job at Kings Cross, cleaning the famous station clock.' The clock is set in the tower, high above the station buildings. It is good to see that the man is wearing a safety rope.

▶ The most famous, and probably the most demanding, structure in Britain requiring continuous maintenance is the Forth Bridge. The painting process reputedly took seven years, and then it was time to start again. Maybe this painter, in a somewhat precarious position, is celebrating the end of one seven-year cycle. In any case, it is a magnificent view of this extraordinary structure.

⬥ A final lick of paint for new colour light signals, possibly at Derby in the 1950s. Signalling maintenance was a specialized activity, quite separate from the permanent way.

⬥ The emergence of the preserved and heritage railway movement introduced new types of railway maintenance workers – the amateur and the volunteer. Here, in the 1960s, a typically mixed volunteer permanent way gang are hard at work on the Paignton & Dartmouth Railway.

ON SHED

Steam sheds, that mecca for railway enthusiasts, are now extinct, except on preserved and heritage lines, yet they were once a vital and very common part of the railway infrastructure, to be found all over Britain. Steam locomotives are relatively simple machines, but they demand regular supplies of water and coal, and constant daily cleaning, servicing and maintenance. The dedicated shed staff catered for all of this. In addition to housing the locomotives when not in use, larger sheds could also undertake heavy maintenance and repairs.

It is March 1967 and the days of steam at Wrexham shed are numbered. On a sunny day, driver and fireman consider a minor problem on their charge, a dirty and worn Class 4 Standard locomotive, No. 75002.

Agecroft, near Manchester, was a large shed, as indicated by this photograph taken in Lancashire & Yorkshire days. The men lined up for the camera appear to be policemen. Perhaps they were responsible for guarding the shed and its many locomotives.

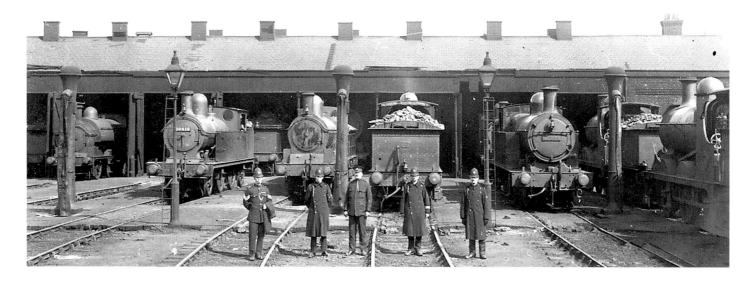

This is Dundee Tay Bridge shed in the early days of British Railways. An elderly 0-6-0 locomotive, probably originally from the North British Railway, is on the turntable.

Ilfracombe in North Devon, seen here perhaps in the 1930s, was a typical small, single-track shed at the end of a branch line. Built to house and service a couple of locomotives overnight, the shed could also look after the banking engine that was required to help heavy holiday trains up the steep incline leading away from the station.

▲ Larger sheds could undertake substantial maintenance and repairs, and were equipped with cranes and other heavy engineering facilities. Here, in Gateshead shed, a pony truck, the pair of leading or trailing wheels to be found on many locomotives, is being inspected for wear and damage.

▲ Two enthusiasts walk out of the old LNWR shed at Tredegar, South Wales, having made the most of that rare enthusiast's dream ticket, a shed pass. One seems to be busily noting locomotives he has seen, perhaps rarities long out of use, hidden in the shed's darker corners.

▲ Two men struggle with a pair of driving wheels at Barnwood, Gloucester, in February 1963. It is a sunny day, though much of Britain was still covered in snow. In the background, an old LMS Class 4F 0-6-0 locomotive is being coaled by hand.

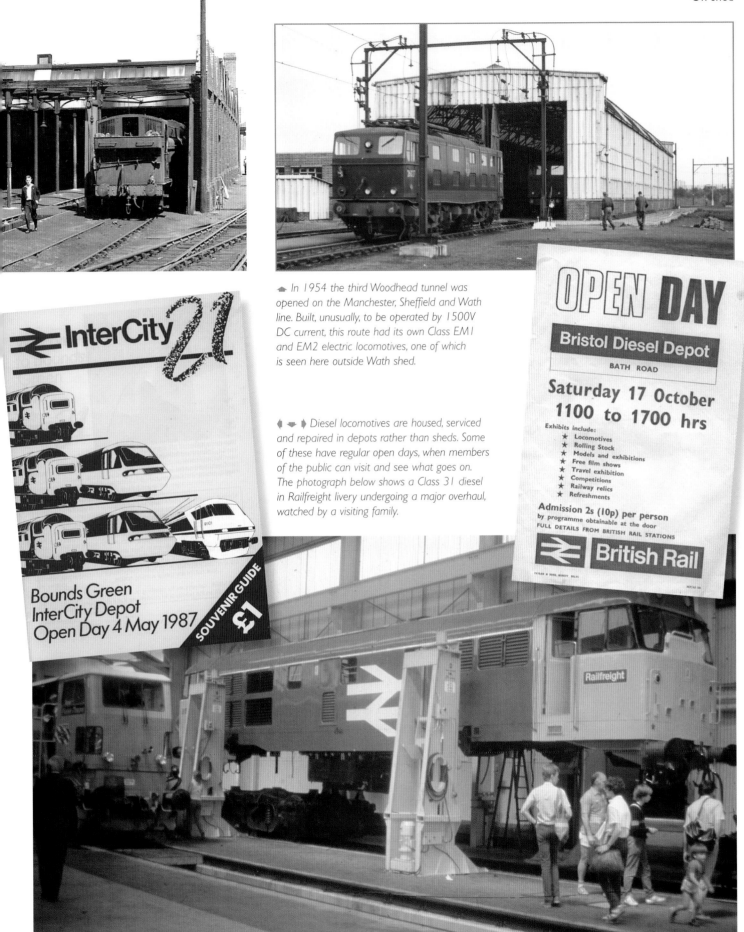

In 1954 the third Woodhead tunnel was opened on the Manchester, Sheffield and Wath line. Built, unusually, to be operated by 1500V DC current, this route had its own Class EM1 and EM2 electric locomotives, one of which is seen here outside Wath shed.

◆ ➡ ◆ Diesel locomotives are housed, serviced and repaired in depots rather than sheds. Some of these have regular open days, when members of the public can visit and see what goes on. The photograph below shows a Class 31 diesel in Railfreight livery undergoing a major overhaul, watched by a visiting family.

InterCity *21*

Bounds Green
InterCity Depot
Open Day 4 May 1987

SOUVENIR GUIDE £1

OPEN DAY

Bristol Diesel Depot

BATH ROAD

**Saturday 17 October
1100 to 1700 hrs**

Exhibits include:
★ Locomotives
★ Rolling Stock
★ Models and exhibitions
★ Free film shows
★ Travel exhibition
★ Competitions
★ Railway relics
★ Refreshments

Admission 2s (10p) per person
by programme obtainable at the door
FULL DETAILS FROM BRITISH RAIL STATIONS

British Rail

AT THE RAILWAY WORKS

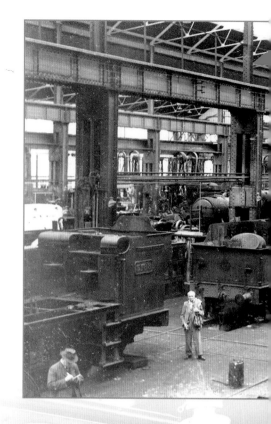

An inevitable legacy of a network built by independent and often competing companies was a large number of works in which locomotives and rolling stock were built and maintained. In addition, there were other works operated by professional railway builders manufacturing for both the home and the export markets, making a total of over 50 across Britain. The first was opened in 1826 and the last early in the Edwardian period. Extensive consolidation took place during the 20th century, many being closed or merged. The 1970s saw everything being brought together as British Rail Engineering, and then, from the 1980s, a break-up prepared the way for privatization and the selling-off of the surviving works to international companies.

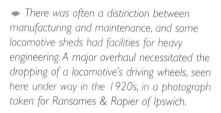

➤ There was often a distinction between manufacturing and maintenance, and some locomotive sheds had facilities for heavy engineering. A major overhaul necessitated the dropping of a locomotive's driving wheels, seen here under way in the 1920s, in a photograph taken for Ransomes & Rapier of Ipswich.

◗ Wolverhampton works was built by the Shrewsbury & Birmingham Railway in 1849 and was later taken over by the Great Western. Here, locomotives in for overhaul are being inspected by some visiting enthusiasts, perhaps during the 1930s.

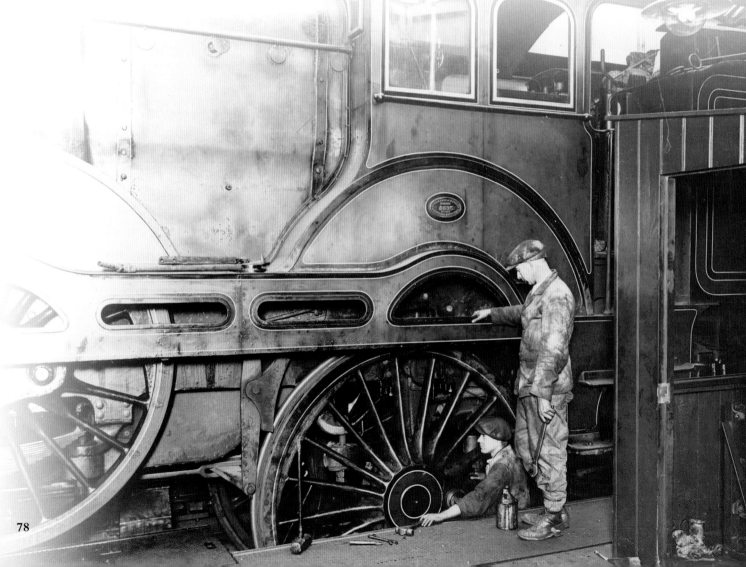

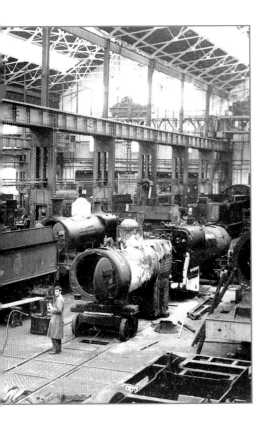

◗ Another Ransomes & Rapier image shows the driving wheels raised back to the floor level for maintenance or repair after the locomotive has been removed by the overhead cranes.

➥ ◗ Doncaster works, one of the biggest, was originally opened in 1853 by the Great Northern and continued to build locomotives until the 1950s. Open days and visits to works were regularly organized by British Railways. This booklet was issued in 1949, when there were 4,800 employees at Doncaster.

Doncaster
Locomotive & Carriage
Works

Locomotives and tenders under construction

BRITISH RAILWAYS

PRINTED IN GREAT BRITAIN

Carriages and goods wagons were built and maintained in dedicated works. This carefully posed promotional photograph shows the Hull & Barnsley Railway's Springhead wagon works in about 1920.

This Edwardian postcard is captioned 'Dinner Time at Wolverton Works'. Opened in 1838 by the London & Birmingham Railway, Wolverton quickly developed into a huge complex, building locomotives and carriages. Turning a remote village into an industrial town, it survived well into the British Railways era.

This publicity photograph of an unidentified wagon works, probably taken early in the 20th century, has been specially planned to show various phases in the construction of wooden goods wagons. The bowler-hatted foreman, standing near the centre, keeps a firm eye on the proceedings.

Dinner Time at Wolverton Works.

CREWE WORKS

BRITISH RAILWAYS

LONDON MIDLAND REGION

.... and what goes on there

CASTING WHEELS

253 01

The HS4000 Kestrel single-engined diesel locomotive was a private venture by Brush Electrical Engineering. Built at Loughborough and completed in 1967, Kestrel was used experimentally by British Rail on a number of passenger and freight routes, with varied results. It remained a unique locomotive and was finally sold to the Russian state railways in 1971. It was broken up in 1993.

Visitors to the open day at Derby's Litchurch Lane works in August 1976 could enjoy, among other things, the new HST 125, the fastest diesel passenger train in the world and still in service more than 30 years later. The family in the foreground certainly seem to be gripped by it.

GENERAL DUTIES

The skills required by people employed in the railway industry have always been extremely varied, and often well outside the limits of a conventional job description. Apart from driving the train, drivers and firemen were responsible for maintaining a locomotive while it was in their care, and this went way beyond the basics of watering and coaling. Shed staff often had even wider-ranging responsibilities. Guards did far more than check tickets, and the duties for station and goods yard staff were endless. Extreme weather or other exceptional circumstances often imposed demands that greatly exceeded the rule book. In return, the railways were generally benevolent employers, with strong trades unions and a variety of social clubs and societies.

➡ *Turning a steam locomotive was part of the daily experience for many drivers and firemen. Many turntables were mechanical, but some required manual operation. Here, in 1957, GWR 6006, 'King George I', is turned at Ranelagh Road, on the approach to Paddington.*

▶ *Though relatively simple in engineering terms, a steam locomotive requires constant attention and maintenance by its crew if it is going to get through its day's work. Lubrication had to be carried out regularly, particularly on the connecting rods and motion.*

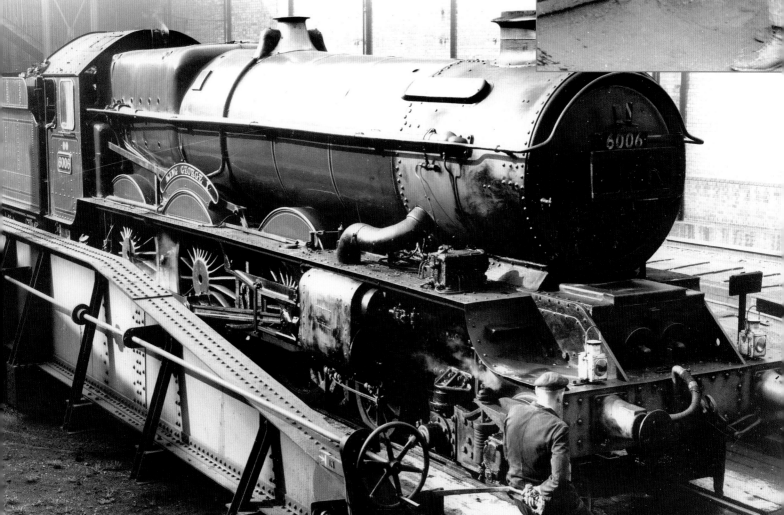

All train crew and shed staff relied on eyes, ears and experience. The condition of wheels or other vital components could be checked by assessing the sound, or ring, when the metal was struck by a long-handled hammer like this one.

The regular use of the oil can was an essential part of the daily life of every working steam locomotive. This carefully posed picture shows a driver attending to the needs of one of London Transport's tank engines.

Volunteers working for preserved railways, like this young man oiling an old GWR locomotive on the Paignton & Dartmouth Railway, have to develop the same skills as railway staff, but often without their years of experience and training.

Cleaning was an important part of the maintenance schedule, and indeed was the bottom of the ladder for trainee firemen. These boys are hard at work on an LNER express locomotive, somewhere in Northeast England in the 1920s. They may well already have been members of their local depot or regional sports club, always a vital part of railway life.

Normanton
Railwaymen's

Sports Club

Member's Card
1947

Buckley & Sons, Printers, Normanton

Throughout a day's work, a locomotive's water tanks or tender needed regular refilling, and most staffed stations were equipped with water tanks, towers or columns. Taking on water was usually the fireman's job. Here, in Oxted, Surrey, in 1952, the driver poses while his fireman does the work.

A locomotive takes on water in the cramped and rather insalubrious conditions at Millwall Junction in the 1950s. The fireman is ready to pull the chain that shuts off the water.

While the driver takes a break, the fireman controls the water chute as he refills this LNER tank locomotive from a lineside tank in a rural location, probably in the 1930s.

Coaling, usually carried out at the shed before the day's work, was often done by hand, though coaling towers were a feature of major sheds and depots. Here, somewhere in the GWR network in the early 1900s, the crew use a tripping trolley to fill the bunkers, with a hose to keep the dust down.

▶ *Many freight and goods yards operated all through the night. In this moody 1930s photograph, the driver of the LNER tank locomotive watches and the shunter leans on his pole while the guard uses his flashlight to check the couplings.*

◀ *The making and drinking of tea, though not really a railway duty, was an important feature of railway life. This 1950s photograph of Midsomer Norton & Welton station, on the Somerset & Dorset Joint Railway, seems to show the signalman seizing a moment before a train arrives to empty his teapot.*

◀ *There is time for the crew to have a chat while GWR County Class No. 1022, 'County of Northampton', takes on water. It is a pity that the location was not noted by the photographer at the time.*

Parcels and many other kinds of urgent freight travelled by passenger train. This shows a busy scene at Bodmin General as the station staff and the guard pile a trolley-load of boxes into the small goods compartment of a 'bubble car', or single-carriage DMU. It is the mid-1960s, shortly before the station and the branch from Bodmin Road were closed.

The handling of unusual freight was just part of a day's work for station staff, though fitting a canoe into a guard's van was not something that had to be done every day.

The front line for many railway employees is the ticket office, where staff have to satisfy the often strange demands of the travelling public. This 1973 photograph, issued by British Rail's public relations department, shows an encounter between a ticket clerk and a young couple in fashionable flowery gear.

↞ On remote lines it was a regular duty for the guard, or sometimes the fireman, to operate points. The Wisbech & Upwell Tramway was a roadside line, with a number of road crossings. Here, in 1950, with the train apparently obeying a road sign, the guard prepares to jump down to operate the points at Outwell village.

↞ The sight of a railwayman leading the Channel Islands boat train through the streets of Weymouth was a familiar one until the tramway serving the quay was closed in the late 1980s, a few years after this photograph was taken.

↞ The exchange of single-line tokens between the train crew and the signalman or a member of the station staff was a feature of branch and rural lines all over the country. This is Haven Street, on the Isle of Wight, in 1959.

◗ *Some photographs raise more questions than they answer. This 1950s image shows two railwaymen posing on a level crossing with a colleague in a self-propelled bath chair. They are all about the same age, so perhaps they worked together until the man in the centre was injured.*

➤ *Another regular duty for the train crew was the opening and closing of the gates at unmanned level crossings, a common event on many rural lines. Here, the locomotive waits and small boys in the grass watch as the gates are closed behind the train.*

L. N. E. R.
ONE
Accompanying Company's Servant.
BETHNAL GREEN to
Rate s. d.
Validity same as Passenger Ticket.
FOR CONDITIONS SEE BACK
0093 0093

☁ *This little photograph is rich in history. The caption on the back says: 'Left to right, chargeman, myself, apprentice, driver, with engine 4522 on trial last week top of Dauntsey Bank, after repairs. 1926.'*

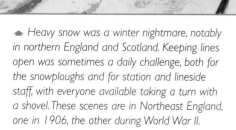

⬆ Heavy snow was a winter nightmare, notably in northern England and Scotland. Keeping lines open was sometimes a daily challenge, both for the snowploughs and for station and lineside staff, with everyone available taking a turn with a shovel. These scenes are in Northeast England, one in 1906, the other during World War II.

▶ Running the railways often required hard physical labour as many structures and pieces of equipment were manually operated. Included in the list was the swing-bridge over the Caledonian Canal outside Fort William, on the Mallaig line, which had to be opened and closed by hand every time a boat needed to pass.

➤ Trade unions became a significant part of railway life from the 1870s, and by 1907 the Amalgamated Society of Railway Servants had over 90,000 members. This led to ASLEF, the NUR and full unionization. The early trade unions were famous for their banners, which were paraded on ceremonial occasions and at conferences. The ASLEF example below is from the Swindon section; the 1960s NUR Christmas card reproduces a 1913 banner.

➤ Photographed in May 1939 at Sandown, on the Isle of Wight, this very mixed group was probably on a works outing. The word 'Stores' on the back of the photograph suggests they are the staff from the Southern Railway's main stores section, responsible for the ordering, warehousing and distribution of the thousands of items required in the daily running of the railways, from major equipment to office furniture, uniforms and tickets. Each British Railways region had a central stores, with smaller local depots around the network, many inherited from the earlier, private companies.

➤ Holidays for employees were arranged by the unions or, sometimes, independent operators. Typical is this 1968 brochure issued by Eurotravel for Belgium, the Netherlands and Italy.

Come to Beautiful
WALES
Cymru am Byth

IN AND AROUND
WALES

DIGAN BAY RESORTS
lorious Sea and Country Holidays

EL BY TRAIN   WESTERN REGION

STATION SCENES

The diversity of railways in Wales, built as they were by a number of companies, has always given them a particular appeal. In South Wales, the coal and valley lines made up one of the densest networks in the world, while elsewhere it was the demands of the landscape that made journeys memorable. Apart from the early route to Holyhead along the north coast, few main lines crossed Wales.

Those that did followed exacting and remote routes. Wales as a whole was famous for its branch lines and country railways; most have been lost, but preservation has brought a few back to life. The photographs shown here have been chosen to reflect those distinctive qualities, particularly of country lines.

The Station–Shrewsbury.

◁ There are a number of gateways to Wales, but the most important is Shrewsbury. From here lines built by different companies spread out in many directions. Standing on a bend in the river Severn, the remarkable 1849 Tudor-style station was designed by TM Penson and is seen here in an Edwardian postcard view.

▽ The busiest route into and out of Wales is via the Severn Tunnel. Completed in 1886, this great feat of engineering provided a direct route into Wales from Bristol. This shows Severn Tunnel Junction in 1964. Waiting in the platform is the scheduled car ferry service through the tunnel.

▽ In the autumn of 1959, at Letterston Junction, on the route from Fishguard to Clarbeston Road, the driver leans out from the train to drop the single-line token.

△ A man and his dog, and the fireman from the GWR tank locomotive resting at the head of a pick-up goods, pose for the camera on the empty platform at Presteigne in the 1960s.

▽ The dense network north of Cardiff included a line westwards from Heath towards Nantgarw. In the 1960s, when this evocative photograph was taken of a pick-up goods passing the former Tongwynlais station, the line was near its end.

▷ Pontllanfraith, like many South Wales towns, had two stations. In 1968 the Low Level station, seen here from a passing enthusiasts' special, had long been closed. The High Level station, on the Tredegar line, was near the bridge visible in the distance.

▽ This busy 1904 scene shows Lampeter station crowded with horses, farmers and spectators while a horse fair special is being unloaded.

▽ Another well-served South Wales town was Maesteg, where there were three stations. Here, in the summer of 1973, a special hauled by a preserved GWR Class 5700 tank locomotive, No. 9642, pauses at one of the former GWR stations.

▷ One of the lost cross-country lines of Wales is the route from Barmouth to Ruabon via Bala Junction and Llangollen, closed in 1965. This is Dolgellau, or Dolgelly as it was in GWR days. A local autotrain rests in the platform, but most of the passengers seem to be waiting for something more substantial.

◁ Wnion Halt was a typically minor rural station a few miles east of Dolgellau on the Barmouth to Ruabon line. In the 1950s, two ladies continue to look out for their train as a locomotive running light passes through.

▽ The train pauses at Bryngwyn, formerly Bryngwyn Halt, on the Llanfyllin branch, and a passenger prepares to descend while the guard watches out for any late arrivals.

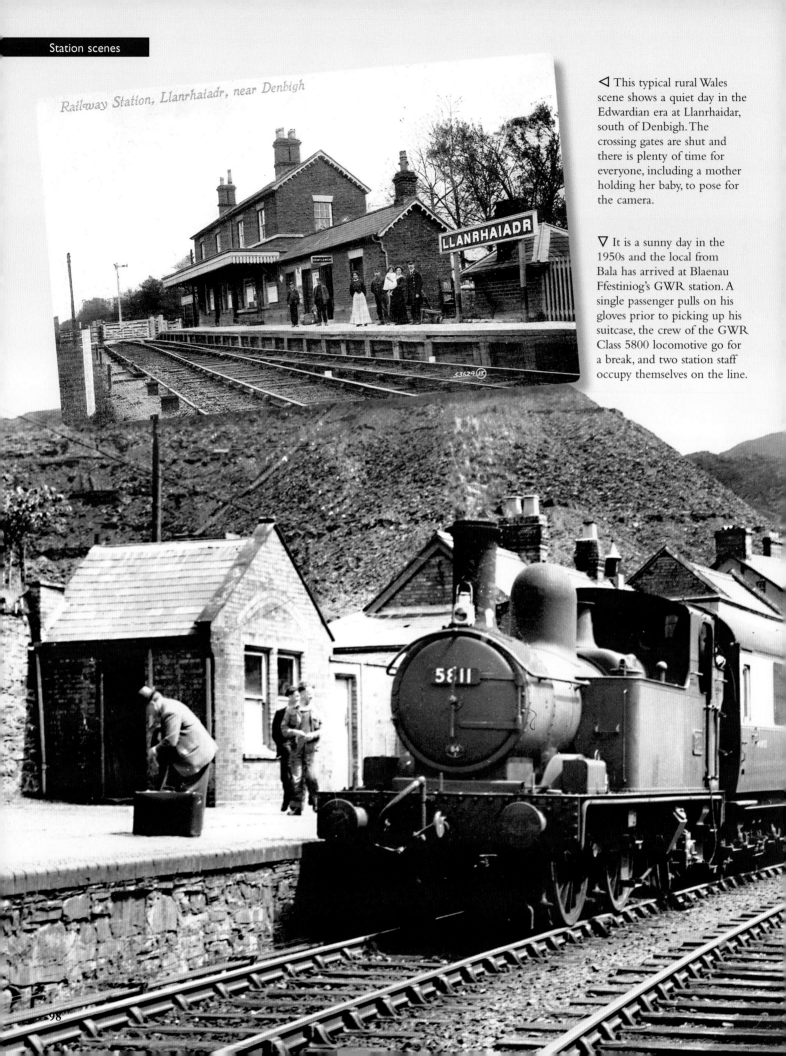

Railway Station, Llanrhaiadr, near Denbigh

LLANRHAIADR

53629 JX

5811

◁ This typical rural Wales scene shows a quiet day in the Edwardian era at Llanrhaidar, south of Denbigh. The crossing gates are shut and there is plenty of time for everyone, including a mother holding her baby, to pose for the camera.

▽ It is a sunny day in the 1950s and the local from Bala has arrived at Blaenau Ffestiniog's GWR station. A single passenger pulls on his gloves prior to picking up his suitcase, the crew of the GWR Class 5800 locomotive go for a break, and two station staff occupy themselves on the line.

△ Llangollen station, set beside the fast-flowing waters of the Dee, is now the terminus of a thriving preserved line. When this photograph was taken in June 1962 it was still a through station on the line from Barmouth Junction to Ruabon. Passengers wait for a train, which the signal indicates is about to arrive, and box vans fill the small goods yard.

▽ In this photograph, taken in June 1975 from the same viewpoint as the one above, the line still looks remarkably intact although it had closed ten years earlier, in 1965. Track, signals and infrastructure have gone, and flowers flourish on platforms and trackbed, but the buildings remain. An enthusiast makes a careful exploration while his friend photographs the scene.

ALONG HOLIDAY LINES

The development of the Welsh railway network was driven primarily by the needs of industry and agriculture, with the emphasis on coal in the south and stone and slate in the north. However, at the end of the Victorian era, holiday and tourist traffic began to grow, thanks in part to the popularity of resorts along the north and west coasts such as Rhyl, Llandudno, Barmouth and Aberystwyth. Also important were Pembroke and the southwest, as well as the many spa resorts in Central Wales, including Llandrindod Wells. Later, the increasing appreciation of mountain scenery and the pleasures of walking opened up Snowdonia, via both standard gauge and narrow gauge lines.

▽ Many Welsh narrow gauge lines were built as industrial railways, but once tourism had become established in Wales, some of the narrow gauge lines began to market themselves as 'toy' railways. Typical was the Talyllyn, which struggled on until 1950, when it was successfully reborn as Britain's first volunteer-run preserved line. This photograph dates from that era.

▷ Railway companies and local tourist offices worked hard to change the image of South Wales from a coal-mining area to a holiday destination. Typical was Barry, a resort whose delights were spelled out in this 1958 leaflet. The railway hub for southwest Wales was Carmarthen, and this route guide was issued to encourage visitors to travel there on the Red Dragon express.

THE Red Dragon EXPRESS — FEATURES OF INTEREST EN ROUTE

See You at Barry

BOOKING OFFICE

GUARD

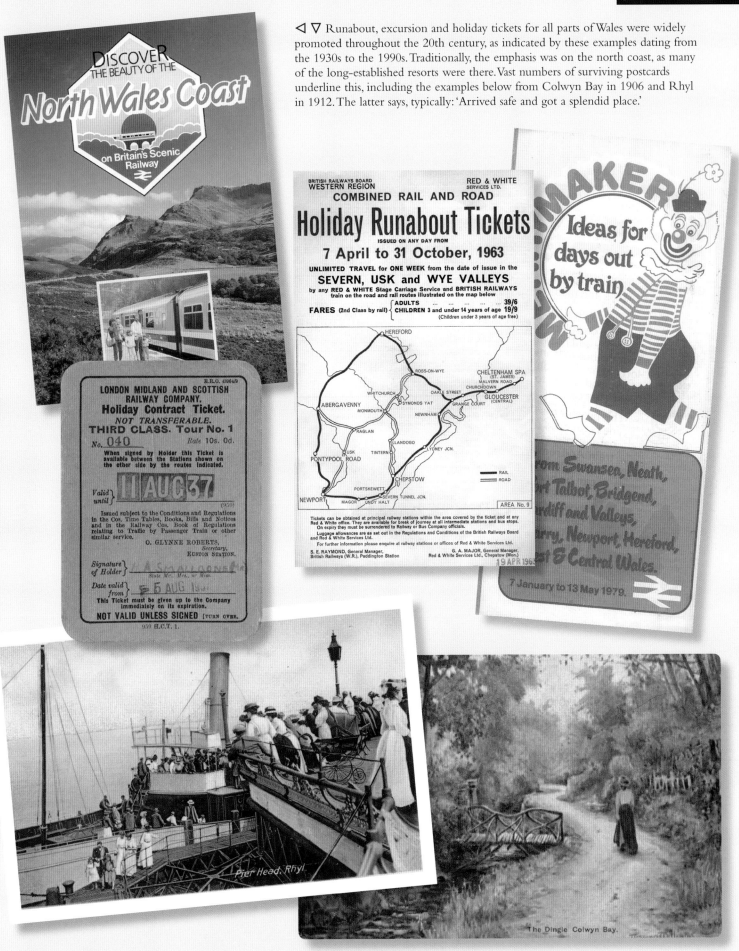

◁ ▽ Runabout, excursion and holiday tickets for all parts of Wales were widely promoted throughout the 20th century, as indicated by these examples dating from the 1930s to the 1990s. Traditionally, the emphasis was on the north coast, as many of the long-established resorts were there. Vast numbers of surviving postcards underline this, including the examples below from Colwyn Bay in 1906 and Rhyl in 1912. The latter says, typically: 'Arrived safe and got a splendid place.'

DISCOVER THE BEAUTY OF THE
North Wales Coast
on Britain's Scenic Railway

LONDON MIDLAND AND SCOTTISH
RAILWAY COMPANY.
Holiday Contract Ticket.
NOT TRANSFERABLE.
THIRD CLASS. Tour No. 1
No. 040   Rate 10s. 0d.
When signed by Holder this Ticket is available between the Stations shown on the other side by the routes indicated.
Valid until } 11 AUG 37
Issued subject to the Conditions and Regulations in the Cos. Time Tables, Books, Bills and Notices and in the Railway Cos. Book of Regulations relating to Traffic by Passenger Train or other similar service.
O. GLYNNE ROBERTS,
Secretary,
EUSTON STATION.
Signature of Holder }
State Mr., Mrs., or Miss.
Date valid from } 5 AUG 19
This Ticket must be given up to the Company immediately on its expiration.
NOT VALID UNLESS SIGNED [TURN OVER.
959 H.C.T. 1.

BRITISH RAILWAYS BOARD
WESTERN REGION   RED & WHITE SERVICES LTD.
COMBINED RAIL AND ROAD
Holiday Runabout Tickets
ISSUED ON ANY DAY FROM
7 April to 31 October, 1963
UNLIMITED TRAVEL for ONE WEEK from the date of issue in the
SEVERN, USK and WYE VALLEYS
by any RED & WHITE Stage Carriage Service and BRITISH RAILWAYS train on the road and rail routes illustrated on the map below
FARES (2nd Class by rail) { ADULTS 39/6
CHILDREN 3 and under 14 years of age 19/9
(Children under 3 years of age free)

Tickets can be obtained at principal railway stations within the area covered by the ticket and at any Red & White office. They are available for break of journey at all intermediate stations and bus stops.
On expiry they must be surrendered to Railway or Bus Company officials.
Luggage allowances are as set out in the Regulations and Conditions of the British Railways Board and Red & White Services Ltd.
For further information please enquire at railway stations or offices of Red & White Services Ltd.
S. E. RAYMOND, General Manager,   G. A. MAJOR, General Manager,
British Railways (W.R.), Paddington Station   Red & White Services Ltd., Chepstow (Mon.)
19 APR 1963

MAKER
Ideas for days out by train
from Swansea, Neath, Port Talbot, Bridgend, Cardiff and Valleys, Barry, Newport, Hereford, West & Central Wales.
7 January to 13 May 1979.

Pier Head, Rhyl.

The Dingle, Colwyn Bay.

North Wales

NORTH WALES

Holiday Pleasure Travel

Croeso i Gymru!
Welcome to Wales!

062

ABERGELE	LLANDUDNO JUNCTION
BANGOR	LLANFAIRFECHAN
COLWYN BAY	PENMAENMAWR
CONWAY	PRESTATYN
DEGANWY	RHYL
LLANDUDNO	

BRITISH RAILWAYS

◁ ▽ Surviving leaflets and brochures reflect the perennial popularity of the North Wales coast, but they should not overshadow other areas, such as Central Wales, with its spa towns and gentle landscape, or Snowdonia, with its magnificently rugged scenery. The Land Cruise, promoted on this 1954 handbill, was one of British Railways' more inventive marketing ideas.

CENTRAL WALES
BY
L. & N.W.R.

To *SEE* North Wales Travel by Train

NORTH WALES LAND CRUISE

A Circular Rail Tour of the most magnificent scenery in North Wales

Mondays to Fridays 14th June until 10th September 1954
(except Monday 2nd August)

(See other announcements for subsequent arrangements)

ITINERARY—RHYL to CORWEN through the VALE OF CLWYD via DENBIGH and RUTHIN, thence through the VALE OF EDEYRNION via BALA LAKE and DOLGELLEY to BARMOUTH where time is allowed for sightseeing. Return along the CAMBRIAN COAST via HARLECH and PORTMADOC, thence via CAERNARVON, MENAI BRIDGE, BANGOR and the NORTHERN COASTAL ROUTE.

OVER 150 MILES OF RESTFUL TRAVEL

Fare	From		Timetable
13/6			a m
13/-	PRESTATYN	depart	9A18
	ABERGELE	„	9A41
	RHYL	„	9 55
	DENBIGH	„	10 25
	RUTHIN	„	10 40
	Barmouth	arrive	12 46 pm
		depart	2 25
Holiday Run about Tickets are not available by this train	Abergele	arrive	5 23
	Rhyl	„	5 31
A—Change at Rhyl	Prestatyn	„	5A40
	Denbigh	„	7A37
	Ruthin	„	8A08

BOOK IN ADVANCE—SEATS ARE LIMITED

One of the many thousands of delighted passengers states : "I cannot think of a more enjoyable way of seeing such marvellous scenery."

POPULAR CAFETERIA SERVICE
A wide & appetizing choice of Refreshments available at nominal prices

Children under three years of age free ; three years and under fourteen half-fares.
For conditions of issue of these tickets, also luggage allowances, see the Railway Bye-Laws, Regulations, Notices and Conditions of Issue of Tickets, etc.
Further information will be supplied on application to the Stations, Agencies, or to F. H. ___, District Traffic Superintendent, Chester Telephone Chester 24680 (Ext. 28)

The Deeside Printing Co., Sandycroft, Nr. Chester.

BRITISH RAILWAYS

May. '54 BR 3...

AFON GLASLYN AND SNOWDON FROM TREMADOC ROAD.

A.1799

Menai Straits from
Llanfairpwllgwyngyllgogerychwyrndrobwll-llandysiliogogogoch
Church | Mary | a hollow | white | hazel | near to | the | rapid | whirlpool | Church | Saint's name | cave | red

THE CAMBRIAN COAST

BRITISH RAILWAYS

See NORTH WALES

The RAILWAY

The BEST WAY

BRITISH RAILWAYS

△ ▷ The Menai Straits bridge, and the nearby railway station with the famously long name, appear frequently in postcards and publicity material. These examples date from 1911 and 1950. Welsh history also played its part in promotional publications: here Harlech Castle is portrayed in a dramatic 1950s image by Jack Marriott for the Cambrian Coast line.

▽ Images of Barmouth Bridge and the Mawddach estuary were much used by the railways and local tourist offices alike. This evocative photograph shows the local for Machynlleth crossing the bridge on a summer evening in 1956, hauled by an old GWR Dukedog locomotive.

ALONG PRESERVED LINES

Opened in 1865 to link slate quarries in the Abergynolwyn region to the coast at Tywyn, the Talyllyn Railway was also a pioneer among narrow gauge lines in the carriage of passengers. Surviving until 1950, the railway was then taken over by a preservation society, which has run the Talyllyn since February 1951. Original locomotives and vehicles, dating back to the line's early days, have been carefully restored, making possible the regular operation of a Victorian train, the oldest complete train in the world. On a Victorian Train Day, passengers and staff dress appropriately, to complete this unique experience.

RHEILFFORDD
TALYLLYN RAILWAY

THE TALYLLYN
**VICTORIAN
TRAIN**

**Your Guide to The Victorian
Train Experience**

▽ The Talyllyn still owns and operates the first two locomotives delivered to the railway, and these are the backbone of the Victorian Train Experience, along with the rake of original carriages. This is locomotive No. 2, 'Dolgoch', bringing its train into Rhydyronen station, where a group of suitably dressed passengers are waiting. 'Dolgoch' started service on the Talyllyn in 1866.

Rheilffordd **Talyllyn Railway**
TYWYN VICTORIAN WEEK
VICTORIAN TRAIN
Tywyn (Wharf) to Abergynolwyn
and back
Subject to Co's Conditions   (cw08
Special Fare   Third Class

▷ The Victorian train can be hired for special occasions and is often in demand for weddings. Here, the Talyllyn Railway's first locomotive, 'Talyllyn', delivered new in 1864, helps to mark the happy day with a special headboard and a white bow. This locomotive, originally built without a cab, was first used during the construction of the railway.

◁ Another view of 'Dolgoch' with the Victorian carriages, and another colour scheme to contrast with the magnificent display of daffodils at Rhydyronen. The Talyllyn's Victorian Train Experience offers a full day's programme of events. In May 1951 this locomotive hauled the first service on Britain's first volunteer-operated preserved line.

◁ △ The Victorian Train Day is always well supported by a great variety of period costumes, in varying degrees of historical accuracy. It is a popular event for children, and Queen Victoria – sometimes accompanied by John Brown – makes a regular appearance at Tywyn station.

ON LESSER LINES

INDUSTRIAL RAILWAYS

The earliest railways were industrial lines, mostly serving mines and quarries. These became the basis of a huge national network of standard and narrow gauge lines built to serve industries as diverse as minerals, iron and steel, chemicals, shipyards and engineering, gas and waterworks, breweries and distilleries, paper, oil and petrol, timber and agriculture. Colliery and mineral lines were the most important and the most long-lasting, many remaining in use until the end of the 20th century. Industrial railways, often privately owned, cheaply built and not always connected to the mainline network, were usually operated by locomotives designed for that purpose, while for drivers and staff it was all a much more basic experience than working on a main line.

LIGHT RAILWAY
BRENDON HILL MINES.   No 8.

⬆ An unusual group pose in front of a Manning Wardle locomotive at an ironstone quarry in the early 1920s. A distinguished-looking man with a fine moustache, elegant Norfolk jacket and Royal Engineers badge – possibly the quarry owner – is flanked by driver and fireman.

⬆ The Brendon Hill iron ore deposits were in a remote part of north Somerset and from the 1850s various railways were built to serve them. This photograph shows a rather primitive narrow gauge line, with everyone, including the smartly dressed man in the centre, posing for the photographer.

▶ Steam survived on industrial lines long after it had vanished from the main line. Here, in March 1972, an elderly Hunslet locomotive shunts coal wagons at Pontardulais in South Wales, under the careful control of a colourfully dressed driver.

The Brymbo Steel Works near Wrexham, set up in 1793, was closed in 1990. It had a massive railway network. This BTH diesel locomotive, 'Hope', poses with a group of workers in 1957.

A classic group – driver with oil can, fireman and manager – captured by the camera with their locomotive, possibly at a quarry.

'Sextus', an 0-6-0 Hunslet industrial locomotive delivered new to a granite quarry in 1896, was still at work in the 1950s, when this photograph was taken.

With their status defined by the style of their clothes, and holding tools to indicate their trades, these men offer an extraordinary insight into life on a colliery railway in about 1900. There is clearly a sense of pride in the job, despite the hard work and the primitive and dangerous conditions associated with many industrial lines.

GOODS TRAFFIC

Until the 1950s, the transportation of goods was the mainstay of much of the railway network. All but the smallest stations had a goods siding or shed, and basic goods-handling facilities. Bulk cargoes like coal, minerals, bricks, oil and petroleum, chemicals, cement, foodstuffs and agricultural products carried by dedicated trains were the backbone of the system. Equally important were the carriage and distribution of local traffic on scheduled mixed goods trains via a nationwide network of freight yards catering for the needs of everything from local businesses to the village shop. Distribution beyond the station or goods yard was carried out by fleets of railway-owned lorries. By the 1960s much of this traffic had been lost to the roads, and the freight network withered away, leaving only bulk cargo and container traffic.

➡ Against the backdrop of a towering railway warehouse crowned by a water tank, an excavator loads spoil onto a standard wooden-plank wagon. The location is unrecorded, but it is a scene typical of railway life throughout Britain during the 1950s.

Beneath St Pancras station in London a vast warehouse looked after the needs of the brewing industry, particularly in the Burton area. This 1958 British Railways publicity photograph shows this giant beer cellar. It is now the passenger waiting area for the International station.

LONDON & NORTH EASTERN RAILWAY

NORTH EASTERN AREA

GOODS MOTOR FACILITIES

NORTHERN SCOTTISH AREA

SOUTHERN

SCOTTISH AREA

NORTH EASTERN AREA

LONDON & NORTH EASTERN

SOUTHERN AREA

THE **L.N.E.R. RAIL-ROAD LINK** BETWEEN CITY, VILLAGE AND FARM

All over Britain men were working in shifts night and day in freight yards and goods sheds to maintain the smooth flow of merchandise around the network. This nocturnal scene is in a busy Great Central Railway goods shed.

It is the summer of 1960 and in the goods yard at Rickmansworth Church Street station, in Hertfordshire, a locomotive waits to shunt coal wagons while the local coal merchant braces himself for filling the sacks stacked on his lorry.

111

Midland and Great Northern Railways Joint Committee.

FRUIT.

From **TURROW**

To LEICESTER, Mid. Rly.

Via PETERBORO' | TRANSHIPS |

BY PASSENGER TRAIN.

☛ There were many seasonal and specialized cargoes carried by the railways, in particular foodstuffs. The cider industry in Herefordshire was dependent upon the railway for the delivery of cider apples, here being shovelled out of open wagons in the 1950s.

☛ In 1911 a general transport strike in the Liverpool area disrupted traffic for 72 days. The army was brought in to ensure the movement of essential cargoes such as coal. Here, a group of soldiers pose for the camera while unloading supplies at Formby Power Station, Lancashire.

◀ In this Edwardian view of Axbridge station, in Somerset, the platform is piled with boxes of soft fruit ready to be loaded. Meanwhile, all work has stopped for the photographer.

◆ *In some places even the pubs relied on the railways for their beer. In this 1950s photograph the landlady looks on anxiously as her weekly supplies are unloaded.*

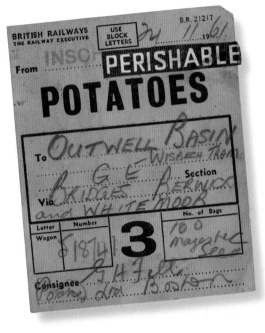

➡ *Rudgwick, near Horsham in West Sussex, was a typical small country station on a rural line yet, as this photograph shows, it had its own goods sidings, seen here filled with laden wagons.*

```
FISH
by PASSENGER TRAIN                    O. 6054
LONDON & NORTH EASTERN RAILWAY.
                    Date
From LOWESTOFT CENTRAL

TO  HASTINGS
         S.E. Section    SOUTHERN Coy.
VIA SPITALFIELDS, EAST LONDON LINE
         and HITHER GREEN

Consignee ...........
Owner and
No. of Wagon ...........    Total
                            Sheets ...........
```

➡ *Box wagons stand ready in the goods yard at Wisbech East, Cambridgeshire, while a variety of horse-drawn vehicles wait to be unloaded. In the meantime the railway staff and wagon drivers stand in line for the camera.*

Despite his slightly unusual clothing, this man has been selected to demonstrate the use of the bussing block, a shoe used to brake individual wagons during shunting. This rather hazardous procedure was photographed somewhere in Northeast England.

All docks were dependent upon their railway connections, and many dock railway networks survived into the 1970s. This shows a Port of London Authority saddle tank locomotive hauling a line of box wagons across a road bridge in the Millwall docks complex in 1961. The younger spectators watch the camera rather than the train.

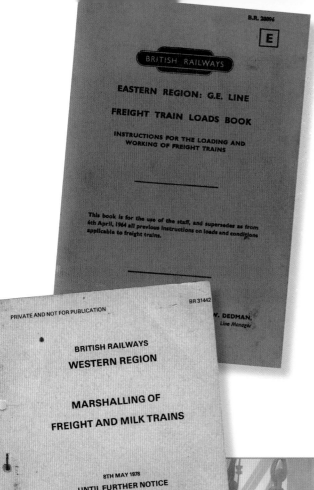

◗ Goods yards were busy places with constant activity as wagons were marshalled into their correct trains. Much of the work was manual, requiring dedication, skill and strength. In this posed photograph a railwayman waits to operate the points, while resting on a pole used to couple and uncouple wagons.

➥ All kinds of cargoes were transported to and from Britain's docks by the railways, and in time of war they became a lifeline for the nation. Here, in January 1942, a Railway Operating Department locomotive bound for Persia is loaded onto a merchant vessel in Newport docks, South Wales, while a surprising number of men look on.

NARROW GAUGE RAILWAYS

In the 19th century, narrow gauge railways were built largely for industrial purposes, with the majority serving quarries and mines in areas where demanding geography and costs ruled out standard gauge lines. Primarily associated with Wales, they were nonetheless to be found in most parts of the United Kingdom. Gauges varied from around 15in on miniature lines to about 4ft. Later, the focus shifted and as many of the old industrial lines began to close, others – including some miniature lines – were adapted, or rebuilt, to serve the needs of tourism. This pattern was maintained through the 20th century, with some of the famous old railways being brought back to life as preserved lines.

➡ A number of independent narrow gauge and miniature lines carried mail, and stamped it accordingly. This railway letter, issued to mark the start of decimal currency in 1971, was carried on the Ravenglass & Eskdale Railway, in Cumbria.

◀ Opened as a 2ft 9in gauge mineral line in 1873, the Ravenglass & Eskdale had a chequered career. From 1915 it was completely rebuilt by WJ Bassett-Lowke as a 15in gauge tourist line. It has remained so ever since, helped by volunteers such as this cheerful pair.

➡ The R&E has a stable of famous locomotives, the oldest of which is 'River Irt'. Seen here on the turntable, this was built in 1894 by Sir Arthur Heywood and is the oldest working 15in gauge locomotive in the world.

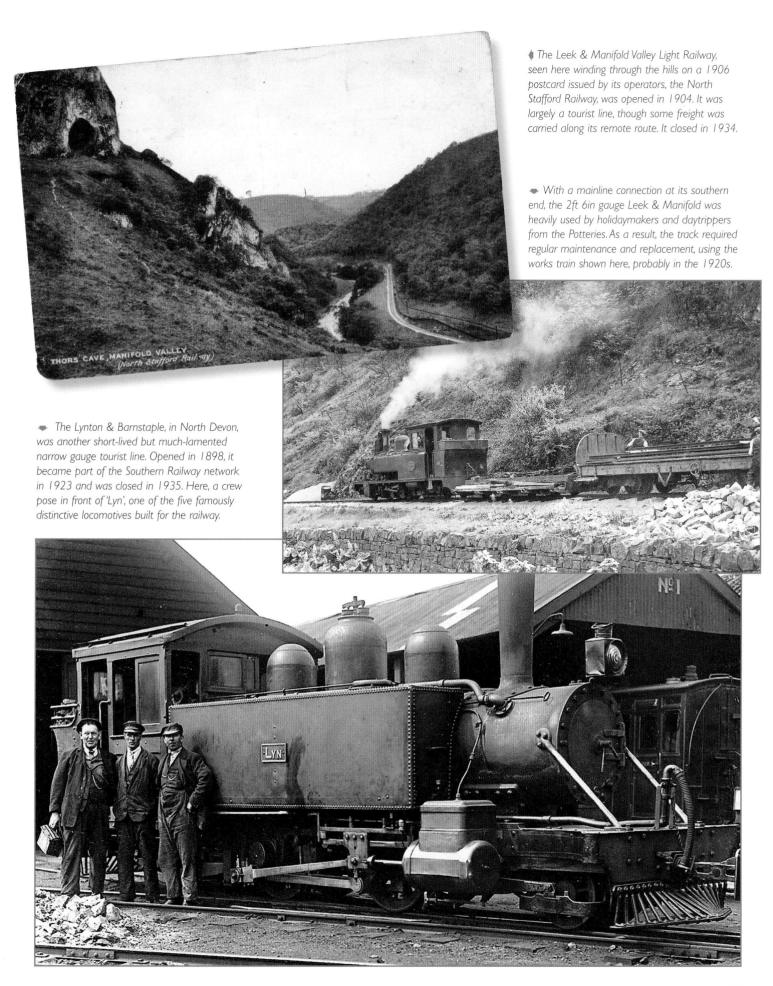

The Leek & Manifold Valley Light Railway, seen here winding through the hills on a 1906 postcard issued by its operators, the North Stafford Railway, was opened in 1904. It was largely a tourist line, though some freight was carried along its remote route. It closed in 1934.

With a mainline connection at its southern end, the 2ft 6in gauge Leek & Manifold was heavily used by holidaymakers and daytrippers from the Potteries. As a result, the track required regular maintenance and replacement, using the works train shown here, probably in the 1920s.

THORS' CAVE, MANIFOLD VALLEY
(North Stafford Railway)

The Lynton & Barnstaple, in North Devon, was another short-lived but much-lamented narrow gauge tourist line. Opened in 1898, it became part of the Southern Railway network in 1923 and was closed in 1935. Here, a crew pose in front of 'Lyn', one of the five famously distinctive locomotives built for the railway.

↑ The miniature Fairbourne Railway was opened in 1890 to serve a building project on the Mawddach estuary, near Barmouth, in northwest Wales. It soon became a tourist line and was rebuilt to a 15in gauge from 1916. Originally all trains were horse-drawn, and in 1990 some horse-drawn services operated to mark the line's centenary.

▶ The 15in gauge Fairbourne line was steam-operated from the start and has remained so ever since. In the 1980s it was rebuilt to a slightly narrower gauge, necessitating new locomotives. On a June day in 1952 a Holiday Fellowship group, staying nearby, enjoy a special outing on the railway.

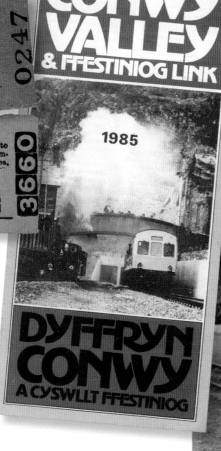

1985

FESTINIOG RAILWAY   74064.
THE LADY STATIONMASTER, AT TAN-Y-BWLCH.

▶ Built as a horse-operated slate line in mid-Wales, the Festiniog Railway opened in 1836. Steam traction started in 1863. By the late 1800s much of the revenue came from passenger carrying. Closed in 1946, it reopened as a preserved line in 1954. The card celebrates its well-known lady stationmaster, while the British Rail leaflet marks the railway's return to Blaenau Ffestiniog.

◀ The Talyllyn Railway, built to connect the Abergynolwyn slate quarries with the sea at Tywyn, was opened in 1866. When it closed in 1950, it was taken over by a volunteer-based preservation society, the first of its kind in Britain. Here, in the early years of preservation, two smartly dressed volunteers are getting to grips, a bit nervously, with a petrol-driven locomotive.

▶ Another 1950s photograph captures the particular flavour of the Talyllyn. A small girl, to the amusement of her mother, is clearly totally enthralled by the sight of locomotive No. 2, 'Dolgoch', an 1866 original.

SNOWDON MOUNTAIN RAILWAY
ONE DOG
ACCOMPANYING PASSENGER
RATE 2/6
NOT TRANSFERABLE
FOR CONDITIONS SEE OVER
0714
8151—Williamson, Printer, Ashton

The Mountain Railway, Snowdon NORTH

◆ *The Snowdon Mountain Railway, Britain's only Abt rack and pinion line, was opened in 1896. It runs from Llanberis to Snowdon's summit. Here, perhaps in the 1950s, an ascending train waits in a passing bay. The crew chat and tinker with the locomotive while the passengers enjoy the view from the open-sided carriage.*

◆ *The Vale of Rheidol Railway opened between Aberystwyth and Devil's Bridge in 1902. At first it carried both minerals and passengers, but it soon became primarily a tourist line. This card, showing scenery typical of the line, was sent from Devil's Bridge, the inland terminus, in 1932 by someone having 'a marvellous time'.*

VALE OF RHEIDOL
NARROW GAUGE RAILWAY

BRITISH RAIL (M)
ABERYSTWYTH DAY
TO RETURN
DEVILS BRIDGE & BACK
Lein Fach Cwm Rheidol (4303)

THE ONLY STEAM
ON BRITISH RAIL

Advertised Not Transferable
Issued subject to the Regulations and
conditions in the Publications and
Notices of the British Railways Board

Nº 95136

You may retain this
ticket as a souvenir
Gellir Cadw y tocyn
hwn fel swfenir
BR 4533

VIEW ON THE VALE OF RHEIDOL RAILWAY.

◆ *Initially independent, the Vale of Rheidol became part of Cambrian Railways in 1913. From 1922 it was operated by the Great Western and in due course became part of British Railways, until 1988. The photograph shows locomotive No. 7 still in GWR livery in 1953.*

◀ Initially a horse-operated mineral and passenger line, the Glyn Valley Tramway opened in 1874, with its mainline connection at Chirk, near Wrexham. Steam took over from 1885, and the railway continued in service until 1935. This early 1930s photograph shows a typical mixed passenger and mineral train stopped at Pontfadog.

➡ The Welshpool & Llanfair Light Railway, which opened in 1903, was, unusually for Welsh narrow gauge, built for agricultural, general goods and passenger traffic. Operated by the Cambrian Railway, and later part of the GWR network, it closed finally in 1956. In the 1960s the railway's route through Welshpool was still visible, though the track was impassable.

◀ When this photograph of Llanfair station was taken, the Welshpool & Llanfair had only recently opened, staff were posing proudly and everything was in good order – including the locomotive, one of two built for the line. In 1963 the railway reopened as a preserved line, from Llanfair to Castle Caereinion. It has since made its way back to the outskirts of Welshpool.

IN AND AROUND
CENTRAL
ENGLAND

OYAL
EAMINGTON SPA

GWR

STRATED GUIDE
SPA MANAGER,
ION BUREAU,
GTON SPA.

RAILWAY FARES
INFORMATION, TRAIN
SERVICES, ETC., FROM
ANY RAILWAY STATION

STATION SCENES

The railway map of Central England has always been dense and complicated, made up as it is with main lines and big city stations, rural cross-country routes and branch lines. Some of Britain's first railways, such as the London & Birmingham, formed the backbone of this map, and then development continued into the 20th century with the completion of the Great Central and its network. Closures in the 1960s were extensive, affecting both major and minor routes throughout this large and varied region, which reaches from the Welsh borders to East Anglia in the east and northwards from London and the home counties to the Midlands. The legacy of this complex map is a great variety of platform scenes, from busy mainline stations to minor country halts, reflecting many aspects of railway life in the 20th century.

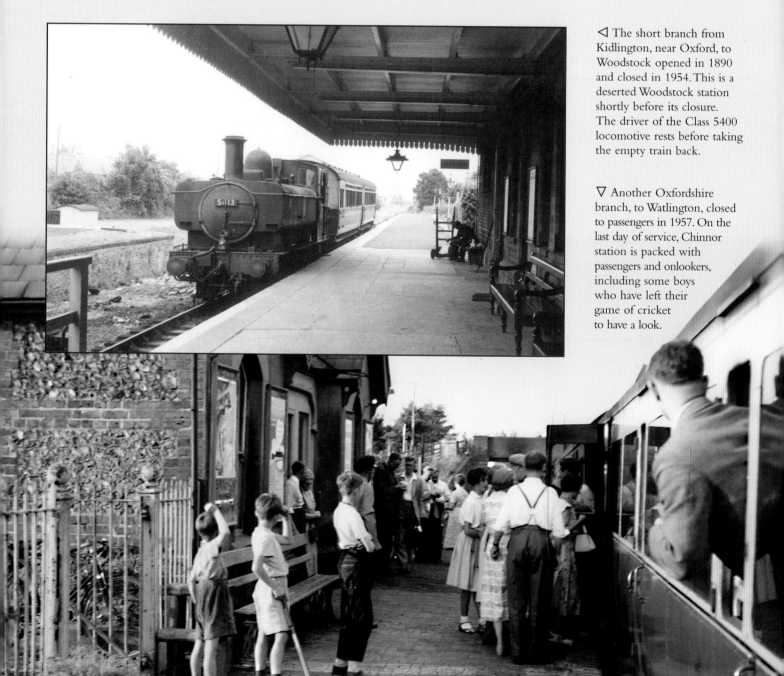

◁ The short branch from Kidlington, near Oxford, to Woodstock opened in 1890 and closed in 1954. This is a deserted Woodstock station shortly before its closure. The driver of the Class 5400 locomotive rests before taking the empty train back.

▽ Another Oxfordshire branch, to Watlington, closed to passengers in 1957. On the last day of service, Chinnor station is packed with passengers and onlookers, including some boys who have left their game of cricket to have a look.

△ A lady waves the train away on the little platform at Bradwell station, on the Newport Pagnell branch, while the driver watches for the guard's signal. It is 1964 and closure is imminent. Someone has written 'Marples Must Go' on the noticeboard. It was a vain hope.

△ Brill, in Buckinghamshire, was the remote terminus of a branch that started life as an agricultural line in the 1870s. Taken over by the Metropolitan & Great Central in 1906, it became the most distant outpost of London's commuter network. Never busy, it closed in 1935.

▷ The Midland Railway built a rural line from Harpenden to Hemel Hempstead. It had an uneventful life. Beaumont's Halt, seen here derelict but still with its nameboard, was an intermediate station.

◁ A busy scene at Northampton Castle station in August 1964, with a crowd of enthusiasts waiting for the departure of LMS Jubilee Class No. 45654, 'Hood'. Castle station served the line northwards to Market Harborough.

▽ Beneath a threatening sky, a member of Olney's station staff braves the rain on the empty platform to watch a locomotive and brake van pass through. Olney was on the rural route from Bedford to Northampton and Towcester.

▽ Accompanied by a friendly member of staff, a young trainspotter has gone onto the forbidden territory of the platform slope at Stratford-upon-Avon in the 1950s to get a closer look at the GWR Castle Class locomotive, No. 5070, 'Sir Daniel Gooch'.

△ While small boys and enthusiasts look on excitedly, a young man sits casually on his case at Birmingham New Street, watching, for want of anything better to do, the LMS Royal Scot locomotive, No. 46137, 'The Prince of Wales's Volunteers (South Lancashire)'.

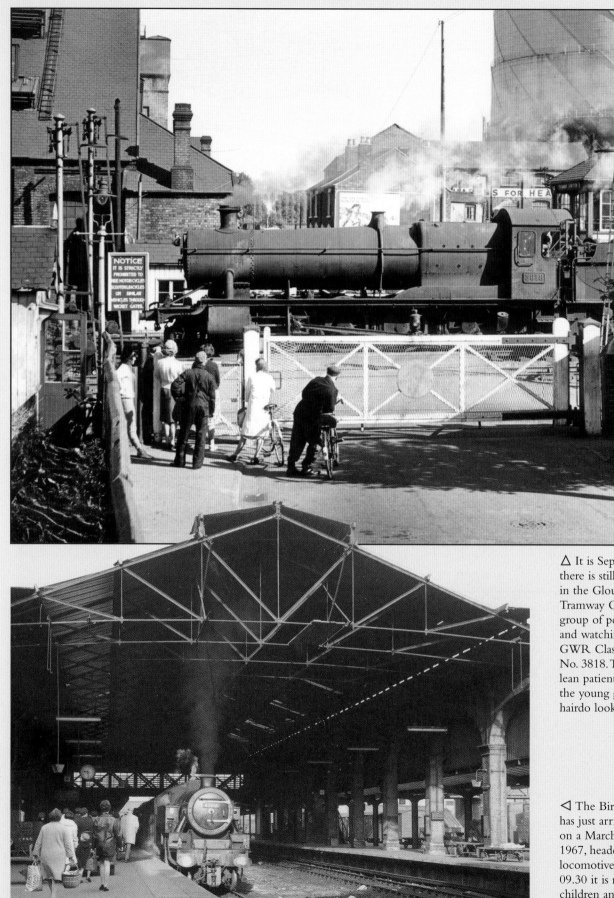

△ It is September 1964 and there is still steam to be seen in the Gloucester area. This is Tramway Crossing, and a small group of people are waiting and watching the passage of a GWR Class 2800 locomotive, No. 3818. The two cyclists lean patiently on their bikes; the young girl with a 1960s hairdo looks bored.

◁ The Birkenhead train has just arrived at Chester on a March morning in 1967, headed by a Class 4MT locomotive, No. 42616. At 09.30 it is mostly women, children and older men who are making their way along the platform.

△ On a May afternoon at Grantham, Lincolnshire, in 1975 just a few people are waiting for the Kings Cross train, entering the station behind a Deltic diesel, No. 55011, 'The Royal Northumberland Fusiliers'. The man in the foreground with a dog, probably there to meet someone off this train from Newcastle, looks unimpressed. The locomotive was withdrawn in 1981 and scrapped.

△ A small boy has a chat, in August 1958, with the driver of this Class 2MT locomotive, No. 41285, at Braunston London Road station, on the line from Weedon to Leamington Spa. A week later the line closed to passengers.

◁ In May 1959 an elderly passenger walks slowly away from Uppingham station, Rutland, while the locomotive rests between duties on this quiet branch line.

◁ Thrapston, in the heart of the Midlands stone country, was well served with two stations. This is Bridge Street, on the old LNWR line. It is a quiet day in May 1964, and soon the station will be closed, along with so many of the rural routes in this area.

▷ Early morning on a sunny day in Nottingham Victoria in 1959, and a wheel-tapper and his colleague, seated on an old Great Central Railway bench on an otherwise deserted platform, are watching the departure of the 07.20 Leek-to-Cleethorpes train.

▽ A shaft of sunlight, an old bench that has lost its iron nameplate, and an evocative display of carefully arranged period posters enliven the empty platform at Loughborough station in August 1946.

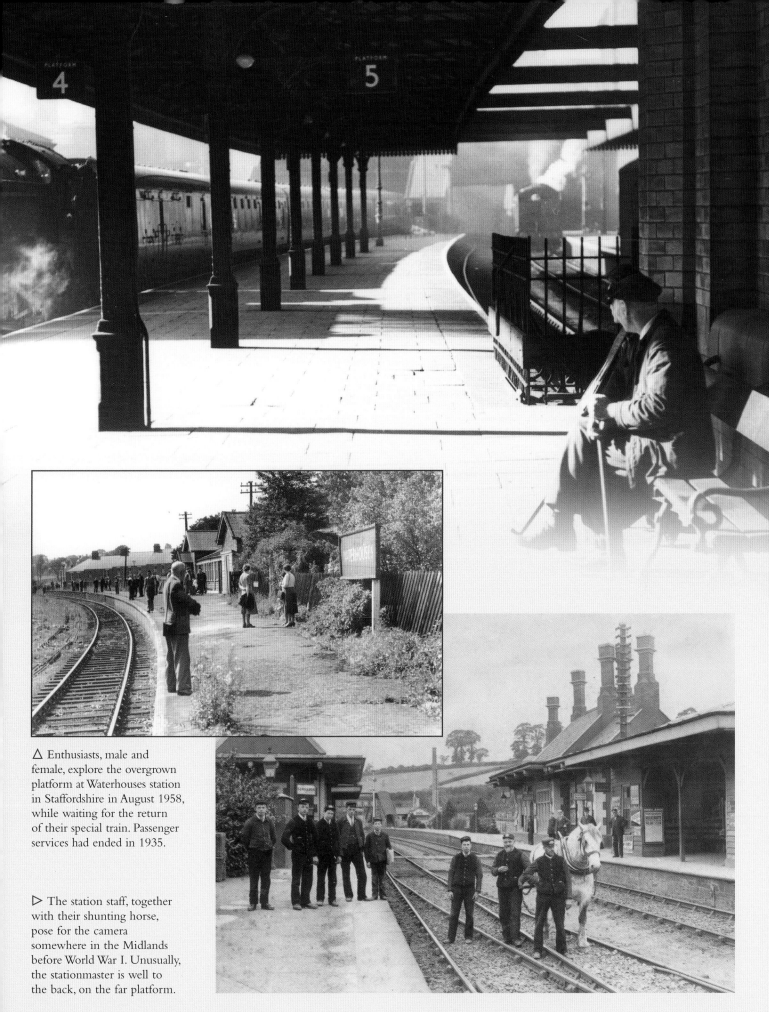

△ Enthusiasts, male and female, explore the overgrown platform at Waterhouses station in Staffordshire in August 1958, while waiting for the return of their special train. Passenger services had ended in 1935.

▷ The station staff, together with their shunting horse, pose for the camera somewhere in the Midlands before World War I. Unusually, the stationmaster is well to the back, on the far platform.

131

ALONG HOLIDAY LINES

The heart of England is not traditionally regarded as a holiday region. Yet its broad spread, from the Welsh borders towards Lincolnshire and East Anglia, incorporates many places and areas popular with holidaymakers and others in pursuit of leisure and relaxation. These include the rivers Wye, Severn and Thames, memorable landscape features, famous walking areas and a rich choice of buildings with important historical associations. Some of the main towns may be better known for their industrial history, but they are all close to attractive countryside, made accessible throughout railway history by the running of excursion trains. Indeed, the first ever railway excursion was organized by Thomas Cook in Leicestershire. With its dense railway network, Central England has long been the home of the day outing.

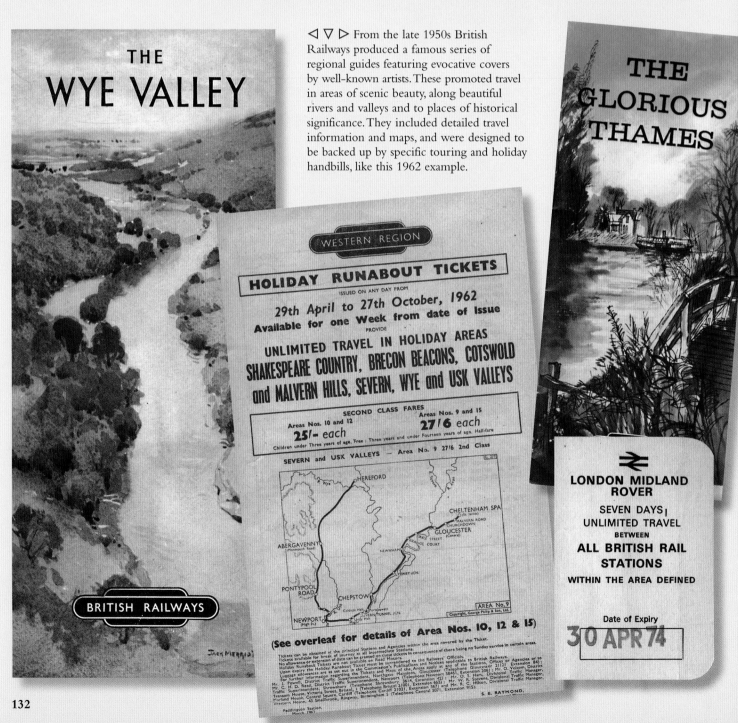

◁ ▽ ▷ From the late 1950s British Railways produced a famous series of regional guides featuring evocative covers by well-known artists. These promoted travel in areas of scenic beauty, along beautiful rivers and valleys and to places of historical significance. They included detailed travel information and maps, and were designed to be backed up by specific touring and holiday handbills, like this 1962 example.

THE WYE VALLEY

BRITISH RAILWAYS

WESTERN REGION

HOLIDAY RUNABOUT TICKETS

ISSUED ON ANY DAY FROM

29th April to 27th October, 1962
Available for one Week from date of Issue

PROVIDE

UNLIMITED TRAVEL IN HOLIDAY AREAS

SHAKESPEARE COUNTRY, BRECON BEACONS, COTSWOLD
and MALVERN HILLS, SEVERN, WYE and USK VALLEYS

SECOND CLASS FARES

Areas Nos. 10 and 12
25/- each

Areas Nos. 9 and 15
27/6 each

Children under Three years of age, Free : Three years and under Fourteen years of age, Half-fare

SEVERN and USK VALLEYS — Area No. 9 27/6 2nd Class

(See overleaf for details of Area Nos. 10, 12 & 15)

THE GLORIOUS THAMES

LONDON MIDLAND ROVER

SEVEN DAYS
UNLIMITED TRAVEL
BETWEEN

ALL BRITISH RAIL STATIONS

WITHIN THE AREA DEFINED

Date of Expiry

30 APR 74

▽ Following a new idea established by the LNER in 1933, the LMS introduced its first camping coaches, or caravans as they called them, in 1934 and within a few years they had spread to many holiday locations in England, Wales and Scotland. Here, in the late 1930s, a family arrives for their week on a quiet, rural siding.

◁ ▽ ▷ British Rail continued to produce stylish and distinctive regional promotional material right up to the end, maintaining a long-established tradition. Much of this, as always, featured areas of natural beauty, such as the Cheddar Caves, now inaccessible by train. Also important were short day excursions; this 1953 handbill advertises trips to Oxford from nearby places.

DISCOVER THE BEAUTY OF THE

Malvern Country

on Britain's Scenic Railway

Supported by the Countryside

THE CASTLE & DINHAM BRIDGE LUDLOW

TO THE CHEDDAR CAVES

BY BRITISH RAILWAYS

THE HOME OF PREHISTORIC MAN

CEMENT
B/R (H.D.)   PLEASE RETAIN THIS BILL FOR REFERENCE   C 156/R. (H.D.)

EXCURSIONS WEDNESDAYS and SATURDAYS
1st SEPTEMBER 1953 until further notice
TO OXFORD (GENERAL STATION)

FROM	Third Class Return Fare	OUTWARD		RETURN Same Day	
		Depart	OXFORD Arrive	OXFORD Depart	Due Back
BICESTER (London Road)	s. d. 2/-	p m 12 52 or 2 17	p m 1 16 2 39	p m 5 18 6 53 or 10 38	p m 5 40 7 17 11 3
BLETCHLEY	4/6	p m 12 10 or 1 36	p m 1 16 2 39	p m 5 18 6 53 or 10 38	p m 6 24 8 2 11 42
CLAYDON	2/9	p m 12 35 or 2 0	p m 1 16 2 39	p m 5 18 6 53 or 10 38	p m 5 58 7 35 11 19
LAUNTON	2/3	p m 12 47 or 2 12	p m 1 16 2 39	p m 5 18 6 53 or 10 38	p m 5 45 7 22 11 8
MARSH GIBBON & POUNDON	2/6	p m 12 40 or 8	p m 2 39	p m 6 53	p m 5 50 7 27
SWANBOURNE	3/9	p m 12 20 or 1 46	p m 1 16 2 39	p m 5 18 6 53 or 10 38	p m 6 14 7 52 11 33
VERNEY JUNCTION	3/-	p m 12 32 or 1 57	p m 2 39	p m 5 18 6 53	p m 6 2 7 40
WINSLOW	3/3	p m 12 25 or 1 51	p m 1 16 2 39	p m 5 18 6 53 or 10 38	p m 6 9 7 47 11 28

CHILDREN under three years of age, free ; three years and under fourteen, half-fares.

CONDITIONS OF ISSUE
Day, Half-day and Evening tickets are issued subject to the conditions applicable to tickets of these descriptions as shown in the Bye-Laws and Regulations, General Notices, Regulations and Conditions exhibited at stations, or where not so exhibited, copies can be obtained free of charge at the station booking office.   For LUGGAGE ALLOWANCES also see these Regulations and Conditions.
Further information will be supplied on application to Stations, Agencies, or to W. N. ROBERTS, District Passenger Superintendent, Euston House, London, N.W.1. (Telephone: Euston 7070); N. H. BRIANT, District Operating Superintendent, Paddington Station, W.2.; or C. FURBER, Commercial Superintendent, Paddington Station, W.2. (Telephone: Paddington 7000, Extn. "Enquiries" 1 8.0 am to 10.0 pm).
British Railways will be pleased to arrange for a representative to call upon secretaries or organisers respecting these excursions or any other outing.

BRITISH RAILWAYS

Published by the Railway Executive (London Midland Region).
C 156/R (H.D.)   AUGUST 1953   B.R. 35001   STAFFORD, NETHERFIELD

HARDWICK HALL.
"More glass than wall."
Rowthorn & Hardwick Station,
MIDLAND RAILWAY.

△ ▷ The Derbyshire Peak District was well served by train and widely promoted from the late Victorian period. The postcard of Hardwick Hall is from a series issued by the Midland Railway, while the LMS brochure is typical of the 1930s, when walking became increasingly popular. British Railways continued to promote this area, as seen in this 1952 excursions handbill.

CXI/A (H.D.)

COMBINED RAIL/ROAD EXCURSIONS WITH BUFFET CAR FACILITIES
FROM
ST. PANCRAS   ST. ALBANS (City)
LUTON (Midland Rd.)   BEDFORD (Midland Rd.)

SUNDAY 15th JUNE 1952
DOVEDALE
(A FAMOUS BEAUTY SPOT IN DERBYSHIRE)

SUNDAY 29th JUNE 1952
The PEAK DISTRICT

COMBINED RAIL AND ROAD FARES

FROM		DOVEDALE	THE PEAK DISTRICT
ST. PANCRAS	- - -	19/6	21/6
Children		10/6	12/9
ST. ALBANS (City)	-	18/-	20/-
Children		9/6	12/-
LUTON (Midland Road)		16/6	18/6
Children		8/6	11/3
BEDFORD (Midland Road)	-	13/3	16/3
Children		7/-	10/3

The tickets are valid on the date for which issued and by the services specified.
FOR TRAIN SERVICE AND CONDITIONS OF ISSUE SEE OVERLEAF

LIMITED ACCOMMODATION
Tickets can only be obtained from—
THE BOOKING OFFICES at ST. PANCRAS, ST. ALBANS (City), LUTON (Midland
Road) and BEDFORD (Midland Road); or by prior arrangement with Stations
and Agencies.
BOOK IN ADVANCE—
Closing date NOON on the FRIDAY preceding the day of Excursion.

Further information will be supplied on application to Stations, Agencies, or to W. N.
ROBERTS, District Passenger Superintendent, Euston House, London, N.W.1. (Telephone:
Euston 1234.)

BRITISH RAILWAYS

PLEASE RETAIN THIS BILL FOR REFERENCE.

THE Peak District
DOVEDALE
MATLOCK

PRINTED IN GREAT BRITAIN
LONDON MIDLAND AND SCOTTISH RAILWAY

◁ In its early years the Leek & Manifold Light Railway was immensely popular with daytrippers and holidaymakers from the Potteries and other nearby centres of industry. This shows a long and packed holiday train pausing at Beeston Tor Halt, deep in the magnificent scenery of the Manifold valley.

PLEASE RETAIN THIS PROGRAMME FOR REFERENCE   D 279

PROGRAMME of
SUNDAY EXCURSIONS
FROM
BIRMINGHAM
NEW STREET
WOLVERHAMPTON
HIGH LEVEL

WALSALL   DUDLEY PORT
COVENTRY   STECHFORD
TILE HILL   SMETHWICK

PLEASE RETAIN THIS BILL FOR REFERENCE

COMBINED RAIL AND ROAD TRIP
TO
ROBIN HOOD COUNTRY
In conjunction with Trent Motor Traction Co.

SUNDAY 7th JULY

| Inclusive Second Class Return Fare | 18/- | Rail to Nottingham and Motor Coach Tour |

Children three and under fourteen years of age 10/6

BIRMINGHAM New Street
Depart 10.0 a.m.
(Change at Derby)

ITINERARY OF TOUR

12. 1 p.m. — Arrive Nottingham Midland Station by train.
1. 0 p.m. — Depart by Motor Coach from Nottingham Midland Station and proceed northwards via Redhill to the village of Edwinstowe, where a stop is made to visit the "Major Oak," thence to Budby and Thoresby Hall, where a halt of 1½ hours is made. After Thoresby Hall we continue to Carburton Dam, thence through charming country to the old world villages of Norton and Cuckney and on to Market Warsop, Mansfield and Nottingham, arriving approximately 5.45 p.m.
6.45 p.m. — Train departs Nottingham Midland Station for Birmingham New Street arriving 8.15 p.m.

Admission Charges to Thoresby Hall — Adults 3/-, Children 1/6

SPECIAL NOTICE
Tickets can only be obtained at the Enquiry Office, New Street Station. Accommodation is limited and bookings will cease at 12.0 noon on the FRIDAY prior to the tour.

SEE OVERLEAF FOR TRIP TO DOVEDALE

LONDON MIDLAND

PLEASE RETAIN THIS PROGRAMME FOR REFERENCE   L87

PROGRAMME OF
THROUGH TRAINS
TO
HOLIDAY RESORTS
FROM
LEICESTER
LONDON ROAD and CENTRAL
and OTHER STATIONS
IN THE AREA

SUNDAY 12th June to SUNDAY 10th September 1961

FOR DETAILS OF ADDITIONAL TRAINS ON FRIDAYS 4th AND 11th AUGUST AND SATURDAYS 5th AND 12th AUGUST, SEE SEPARATE LEICESTER HOLIDAY PAMPHLETS.

TICKETS CAN BE OBTAINED IN ADVANCE AT STATIONS AND OFFICIAL RAILWAY AGENTS

Information will be supplied on application to Stations, Official Railway Agents, or to the District Commercial Manager, Leicester. Telephone 23841, Extn. 105.

LONDON MIDLAND   PG2/SMR/61

Arthur Gaunt & Sons (Printers) Ltd. Heanor, Derbyshire.

SHAKESPEARE COUNTRY

BRITISH RAILWAYS

Nottingham Goose Fair,

◁ British Railways worked continuously to promote holiday and excursion travel, particularly from the major towns and cities of the Midlands. At the same time they made the most of such famous historical figures as William Shakespeare, and traditional events such as Nottingham's Goose Fair.

ALONG PRESERVED LINES

A relatively late arrival on the preservation scene, the Churnet Valley Railway ran its first trains in 1996. Today it operates over a part of the former North Staffordshire network between Cheddleton and Kingsley & Froghall, with plans to extend the line north towards Leek and south to Alton. The Churnet Valley organizes a regular series of special events and activities. One of the most popular is the 1940s weekend, something that figures in the calendar of many preserved lines. Costumes, often put together with a remarkable eye for detail, old vehicles and a high level of period re-enactment, frequently including live music, make this a memorable weekend. Many of the participants travel around from railway to railway during the season, acting out a variety of 1940s roles.

▷ Nothing sets the 1940s scene better than music, both recorded and live. Here, wearing WRAF uniforms, local singing sensation The Forties Flyers work their way through a familiar but highly evocative routine.

CHURNET VALLEY RAILWAY (1992) plc.
Cheddleton   Froghall
to   to
FROGHALL   CHEDDLETON
              via
RETURN   LEEKBROOK
Issued subject to the Bye-laws, Notices,
Regulations and conditions of the Railway
5262

When The Lights Go On Again
1940's Weekend
at
The Churnet Valley Railway
A Weekend of nostalgia for all the family
25th & 26th April 2009

◁ Choice of costume is a highly personal matter, with a variety of both replica and original clothes on display. Typical is this group enjoying the musical entertainment. Only one person is not in period costume.

CHURNET VALLEY RAILWAY

△ ◁ Hairdo and make-up are just as important as costume.

▷ Rather incongruously, German uniforms seem to be popular, and at this event Consall station was in German hands. Perhaps this officer is reporting the capture via his mobile phone.

▽ Even romance seems to have a period quality as this paratrooper prepares to leave for Normandy or Arnhem.

GOING TO WORK

Railway companies have always courted the business traveller and much has been done over the years to make the most of this important source of revenue, including the provision of special trains, carriages and compartments, dedicated facilities, ticket payment schemes and car hire services. Catering for the needs of commuters, always less appealing to the railways, has also been an essential part of their business since the latter part of the 19th century, despite inevitable problems arising from crowded peak travel, season tickets and spare stock at off-peak times.

☛ Season tickets were first issued in very limited ways in the 1830s, but they did not become common until after World War II. From then their increased use, with the addition of Third Class, was linked directly to the spread of the suburbs.

◀ ☛ Dedicated facilities and First Class comfort and speed featured in railway advertising aimed at the business market. These examples date from just before and just after World War I.

▲ A packed platform at London Waterloo and the grim realities of the daily commute feature, rather surprisingly, in this 1960s photograph issued by British Rail's publicity department.

Kirkby

British Railways
AUTOBRITN PLAN

By
TRAIN & CAR
you
TRAVEL FAR

arrive fresh and relaxed—then drive on
your way—in a latest model car from

THE
VICTOR BRITAIN
RENT-A-CAR SYSTEM

Head Office:
12a BERKELEY STREET, LONDON W.1
Tel: GROSVENOR 4881 (10 lines)
Telex 2-3688

British Rail
Travel Warrants

Travel now—pay later

for the business man

it's a deal quicker
by RAIL

TING—BACK IN A DAY

507 015

Local stations on busy lines have encouraged
suburban development, and they have also been
built in response to changing social patterns. In 1978
a new station was opened at Kirkby, on the Hunts
Cross, Liverpool and Southport network, and it proved
to be immediately popular with commuters – as this
photograph indicates.

THERE AND BACK IN A DAY . . .

SEPTEMBER 19TH 1955 TO JUNE 8TH 1956

TRAINS FOR THE
BUSINESS MAN
(MONDAYS TO FRIDAYS)

TO LONDON

EAST AND WEST
MIDLANDS
SOUTH
* FO. FX. A. B. C.—See notes on back cover.   NORTH

In the 1950s and 1960s British
Railways worked hard to hold on
to the profitable business traveller,
emphasizing speed, comfort, credit
arrangements and car hire.

Officers in the Services have
long been a rewarding part of the
business travel market. Here, in
1939, an army captain enjoys a
cigarette in a First Class carriage.

◀ Identified by his badges of office – the hat, the classic coat, the tightly rolled umbrella and a newspaper – a businessman walks away from the train that has just brought him into Birmingham's Snow Hill station. It is probably a winter's day in the late 1950s or early 1960s, and plenty of former GWR locomotives are still in service on lines into Birmingham from Wales and the West of England.

Red Star Timetable
CARLISLE
11 May 1987–8 May 1988

**You've got a deadline
We've got the lifeline**

▶ This 1957 brochure gives the times of trains from Glasgow suitable for business use, with information on warrants for travel, cheap day tickets, meals and refreshments, and telephone and telegram services. It also uses the famous slogan 'Travel by Train and Avoid the Strain'.

➤ During the 1960s British Railways responded to increasing competition with marketing campaigns that concentrated on the advantages of rail travel, particularly for the business user. Typical is this brochure issued to staff by the North Eastern Region in 1961, identifying the main selling points as Safety, Speed, Comfort, Convenience and Reliability.

THERE AND BACK IN A DAY

17th JUNE until 14th SEPTEMBER, 1957

TRAINS FOR THE BUSINESS MAN

FROM GLASGOW

➤ The Red Star parcels and documents service was set up by British Rail in 1963 to compete with the Post Office's overnight business traffic. It was an express service using passenger trains, and many stations had a Red Star depot or office. This 1988 timetable shows Red Star services from Carlisle. Red Star was sold in 1995 and subsequently closed.

Putting the Customer in the Picture

FACTS ON SELLING RAIL TRANSPORT

NORTH EASTERN REGION

It is an autumn or winter morning in the early 1960s and the concourse at London's Victoria station is crowded. The rush hour might be over, but most of the people in the photograph, taken by British Railways' public relations department, are business travellers. Many seem to be in a hurry, but some are standing and chatting, and it looks as though one or two might even be planning to use the recording booth. For 2s 6d (12½p), they can make a 45rpm record to send as a musical greeting to a friend or relation.

A new generation of high-speed Pullman trains was introduced in 1960, aimed specifically at the business market. This leaflet, promoting the Midland Pullman from London to Leicester and Manchester, was issued in 1960. These stylish trains were composed entirely of First Class and Pullman carriages. Advance booking was recommended.

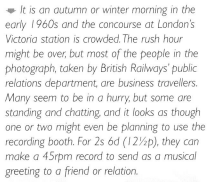

WOMEN & CHILDREN

In the first years of its existence, the railway network would have had little impact on the daily lives of ordinary people. This was soon to change, however, as the potential for travel became increasingly accessible, thanks in part to government control of ticket prices. The result was that domestic life was changed beyond measure, and families came to depend upon the railways not just for work but for shopping, schooling, holidays, social life and so much else. In this way, the railways had more and more of an impact on the everyday lives of women and children, becoming a constant part of the domestic scene and remaining so until the late 20th century.

In the summer of 1981 a London-bound HST 125 roars along the famous stretch of seaside track near Dawlish, in Devon. On the beach, families enjoy the sun, largely oblivious to the passing train. In the foreground a woman and her daughters are on their way to, or from, the beach. Ahead of them a man sits on the wall, the only person actually watching the train.

This British Railways publicity photograph from the 1950s beautifully captures the excitement of the moment as these children set off on holiday. They are, of course, travelling by train, and the journey will be an important part of their holiday experience.

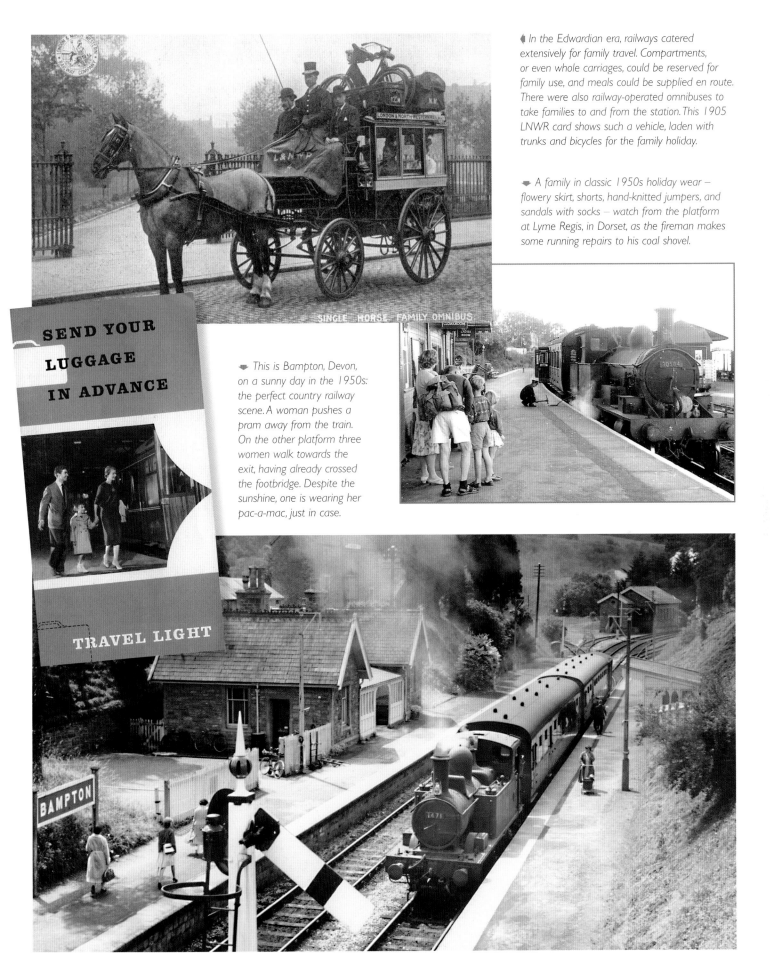

In the Edwardian era, railways catered extensively for family travel. Compartments, or even whole carriages, could be reserved for family use, and meals could be supplied en route. There were also railway-operated omnibuses to take families to and from the station. This 1905 LNWR card shows such a vehicle, laden with trunks and bicycles for the family holiday.

A family in classic 1950s holiday wear – flowery skirt, shorts, hand-knitted jumpers, and sandals with socks – watch from the platform at Lyme Regis, in Dorset, as the fireman makes some running repairs to his coal shovel.

SINGLE HORSE FAMILY OMNIBUS

SEND YOUR LUGGAGE IN ADVANCE

This is Bampton, Devon, on a sunny day in the 1950s: the perfect country railway scene. A woman pushes a pram away from the train. On the other platform three women walk towards the exit, having already crossed the footbridge. Despite the sunshine, one is wearing her pac-a-mac, just in case.

TRAVEL LIGHT

BAMPTON

▶ In May 1962 a neatly dressed family walk smartly towards the exit of Craigleith station. The man, clutching his camera, casts a backward glance at the DMU, which is ready to depart for Edinburgh Princes Street. Neither his wife nor his sons share his interest.

☛ A cheerful porter watches the approaching train from the timber platform of Napton and Stockton station, on the line between Leamington Spa and Weedon. Behind him, a woman in a summer frock holds the pram and her children tightly, to keep them all safe. It is 30 August 1958, two weeks before the line's closure, announced by the poster in the foreground.

GENTLEMEN

⚓ *The driver and fireman of Class A1X Terrier tank No. 32678, resting between regular shuttling up and down the Hayling Island branch, in Hampshire, keep a casual eye on two ladies, perhaps mother and daughter, stepping briskly away from the train. Shopping is clearly in prospect for the two, as they are well equipped with bags. When they are ready to go home, they will, naturally, take the train again. Clothes and hair styles suggest the early 1960s, which means that they would soon have to change their habits: the Hayling Island branch closed in November 1963.*

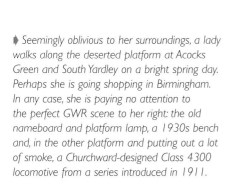

▶ *Seemingly oblivious to her surroundings, a lady walks along the deserted platform at Acocks Green and South Yardley on a bright spring day. Perhaps she is going shopping in Birmingham. In any case, she is paying no attention to the perfect GWR scene to her right: the old nameboard and platform lamp, a 1930s bench and, in the other platform and putting out a lot of smoke, a Churchward-designed Class 4300 locomotive from a series introduced in 1911.*

ACOCKS GREEN
AND
SOUTH YARDLEY

Taking the train

It is the late 1940s and Britain is deep in a period of postwar austerity. Trains are worn out and uncared for, awaiting the brave new dawn of nationalized British Railways. Typical are the locomotive and rolling stock seen here waiting in the platforms at Exeter Central. In contrast to the gloomy surroundings, the two ladies who have stopped for a chat are well dressed in clothes that reflect the latest styles – and a spirit of optimism.

The level crossing in Eastgate Street, Gloucester, just beyond Eastgate station, was famously difficult and sometimes dangerous. Nevertheless, this family, dressed à la mode in the 1960s, are determined to cross without a glance at the train about to depart.

This busy 1959 scene shows Buckingham station, soon after the arrival of the service from Bletchley. Most passengers have made their way over the bridge towards the exit, but one lady had to wait to unload her bicycle from the guard's van and is bringing up the rear.

Dolserau Halt was one of a number of similarly remote stations on the line from Barmouth to Bala Junction. The line closed in 1965. In its latter years the line saw few passengers, but this lady is determined to take the train – despite the broken lamp, battered nameboard and basic shelter.

➥ The caption on this September 1973 photograph says it all: 'Two charming passengers wait at Bath Spa for a return train to Swindon, after a day's shopping.' Let's hope their photographer friend made it back in time from the opposite platform to join them on the train.

➥ Many popular postcards of the Edwardian era featured classic railway and platform scenes, reflecting the part played by trains in ordinary lives. This typical example is titled 'Good-bye Mother' and shows an experience that was by then universal.

PARTY OUTINGS

Group travel has been a feature of railway life since the early days and, until its demise, British Rail continued to promote the benefits of group travel in a range of special brochures, often with enticing covers. The group could be a small party of friends or family members, usually ten or so, or something much larger, requiring a special carriage or even a whole train. Church parties, professional or trade bodies, institutions such as the scouts, and the military were typical users of group travel.

⬤ The leader of an all-male group assembled on the platform at Witham, in Essex, has a discussion with the driver while the old locomotive simmers away quietly. A small boy, presumably having just noted the engine's number, walks back to rejoin the group.

⬤ Hop pickers, notorious for their raucous and often unruly behaviour, travelled in huge groups in special trains. In the 1930s more than 33,000 were transported each year by the Southern Railway to destinations such as Paddock Wood or, here, Faversham. This traffic ended in 1960.

ARRIVAL OF PICKERS AT FAVERSHAM STATION.

This is Achnasheen station on the Kyle of Lochalsh line in the Scottish Highlands in the 1950s, and a group of naval cadets have just arrived at the station in an elegant coach. Teachers, or possibly parents, discuss the arrangements while the signalman looks on.

A mixed-age Edwardian group, dressed in Sunday best and perhaps from a church or similar organization, wait for their train at Camberley & Yorktown station, in Surrey. There is no rush and the photographer has had time to arrange them well, with the leader in the centre.

A group of soldiers pose informally on Redbridge station, near Southampton. One of them is without his cap, but maybe the two sergeants in the front row have not noticed and the corporal behind him has chosen to ignore this breach of regulation. Meanwhile, three boy scouts, clearly part of the same party, work out the journey on a map.

Party Outings by rail

combined tours..

..by rail-road and steamer

BRITISH RAILWAYS
NORTH EASTERN REGION

CHEAP TICKETS

Since the 1840s railway companies have invented many schemes to attract passengers, particularly for off-peak or holiday travel. From the 1950s these became more prolific and ambitious, as British Railways faced ever-increasing competition from road and air transport. The majority of these schemes were aimed at families, but others targeted business travellers, the young and the elderly – the latter particularly in the 1980s. Many emphasized both the cost savings and the pleasures of rail travel. The brochures, leaflets and promotional documents shown here illustrate many of these marketing ideas, including an All Stations pass valid for nine days' unlimited travel, a Three-Destinations ticket, circular tour tickets, and an LMS saving stamps scheme for rail travel.

PLAN YOUR JOURNEYS
BY RAIL
WITH THE AID OF
CIRCULAR TOUR TICKETS

BRITISH RAILWAYS

TRAVEL BY RAIL – IT'S QUICKER

Ask at any L M S Station for full details of the following :—

L M S "Holiday Contract Tickets." Unlimited rail travel in your holiday area **for a whole week for 10/-.**

L M S "Inexpensive Holidays." Hotel or Boarding House accommodation and pleasure trips by rail and road at **inclusive low charges.**

Facilities for Parties. Attractive low rates for parties travelling together on the L M S.

SHOW THIS CARD TO YOUR FRIENDS

The new THREE-D TICKET

AMAZING HOLIDAY BARGAIN

EASE THE STRAIN –
GO BY TRAIN

British Railways

PASSENGER TRAVEL FACILITIES

LMS SAVE-TO-TRAVEL SCHEME

NAME OF HOLDER ....

ADDRESS ....

....

SIGNATURE ....

NOTES.

1 Only the special LMS "Save to Travel" Stamps may be affixed to this card.

2 When completed exchange this card for a 10/- travel voucher thereby securing interest on the 10/- of your accum...

3 The vouchers may ... season tickets) at a ...

4 The holder is reque... safeguard.

BRITISH RAILWAYS (E)

SEASON TICKET No. **2653**

THIRD CLASS RATE B.FRS.1,2...

AVAILABLE BETWEEN

ALL STATIONS
BY BRITISH RAILWAYS

DATE FROM 10 AUG 1959
TO 18 AUG 1959

Signature of Holder
Signature de l'titulaire
Unterschrift des Inhabers

Passport No. 213072 Date of Issue 6 AUG 1959

THIS TICKET IS NOT TRANSFERABLE

British Railways
MIDWEEK THRIFT PLAN

START YOUR HOLIDAY ON
Tuesday Wednesday or Thursday
AND MAKE BIG FARE SAVINGS...

Save up to 7/- in the £ on your rail fare

TAKE A PERIOD
MID·WEEK HOLIDAY RETURN

TUESDAY WEDNESDAY THURSDAY

2nd Class only
6th MAY to 30th OCT. 1958

WESTERN · BRITISH RAILWAYS · REGION

Now lasts a full 12 months from when you buy...

Half-price train travel for ANYONE under 24

And it's still only £10.

This is the age of the train ⇌

ECKERSLEY

FROM 30 APRIL TO 28 OCTOBER 1961

Holiday Runabout Tickets
in all the popular holiday areas

With a Holiday Runabout Ticket you can travel as much as you like throughout the Area, every day while the ticket is valid.
With a Holiday Runabout Ticket you can see — conveniently, cheaply — all there is to be seen within a wide radius of your chosen holiday centre.
You can get your Holiday Runabout Ticket on demand at a principal station, or on 48 hours' notice at any other station, in an Area (12 hours' notice in Scotland).
Children aged 3 and under 14 travel at half-price in most cases.
(Please note that prices of tickets remain the same where, in certain Areas, there are no services on Sundays.)

BRITISH RAILWAYS Ask for full details when you arrive at your holiday centre

Make your pension go a nice long way

THE ROYAL FAMILY

Queen Victoria started travelling by train in the 1840s and links between the royal family and the railways have been maintained ever since. Over the years there have been many royal trains, and the most recent is still in service. The major royal events, such as coronations, weddings, funerals and state visits, have generally had either railway participation or an impact upon the railways in the form of special services. As a result, royalty and the railways is a well-documented subject, with a wealth of interesting images and memorabilia.

➤ *The major royal palaces were served by local stations, some being specially built, others having private areas. The station for Balmoral was Ballater, the end of a long branch from Aberdeen. This card shows George V's arrival at Ballater in 1911, on his first visit to Balmoral as king.*

THE FIRST VISIT OF KING GEORGE V TO BALMORAL
THE ARRIVAL AT BALLATER STATION

Chingford Railway Station, Welcome to Queen Victoria opening Epping Forest to the people.

◀ *This triumphal arch was built at Chingford station to welcome Queen Victoria on the occasion of the handover of Epping Forest, a former royal hunting ground, to the people on 6 May 1882. The Queen declared: 'It gives me the greatest satisfaction to dedicate this beautiful forest to the use and enjoyment of my people for all time.'*

⮕ Royal trains were used extensively by Queen Victoria and subsequent monarchs, and a number of the major railway companies built their own versions. Here, in June 1900, a royal train leaves York for Newcastle, headed by a spotless and suitably decorated NER S Class locomotive.

🔹 Coronations and other royal events have always been hugely popular. Here, in 1911, children from all around Lewes, Sussex, dressed in their Sunday best, are led away from the railway station to take part in local celebrations to mark the coronation of George V.

⬆ On 31 May 1961 a more recent, and more restrained, royal train passes slowly through Clapham Junction on its way to Tattenham Corner for The Derby, headed by a Southern Railway Schools Class locomotive, No. 30926, 'Repton'. For this short journey the royal carriage has been sandwiched between Pullman cars.

Taking the train

➤ In railway terms, a royal funeral was always a momentous event. Here, on 23 January 1936, crowds have gathered at a remote East Anglian level crossing to witness the passing of the royal train carrying the coffin of the late King George V from Wolferton, the station for Sandringham, for the lying-in-state in Westminster Abbey.

▶ King Edward VII also died at Sandringham, on 6 May 1910, and his body was similarly transported to London by train for the lying-in-state and thence to Windsor for the funeral on 20 May. This shows the coffin being taken from the train at Windsor station and about to be loaded onto the gun carriage.

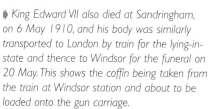

FUNERAL PROCESSION
OF HIS LATE MAJESTY KING EDWARD VII.
Windsor, Removing the Coffin from the Train. — LL.

Visit of H.R.H. PRINCE GEORGE to the works of the HUNSLET ENGINE © LTD. Leeds, May 1931. In background one of eight engines built for the Southampton Graving Dock to the order of Messrs John Mowlem & Co. Ltd., London.

◀ *Railway history is rich with royal occasions and special visits. The Hunslet Engine Works in Leeds received two royal visits in 1931, from Prince George of Denmark in March and from HRH Prince George in May. This shows the latter visit, with Prince George in conversation with Hunslet's managing director, Alexander Campbell. The company's engineer, John Alcock, is on the left.*

▶ *The staff at Wolferton station have been very attached to the royal family over several generations. In December 1952 they are hard at work decorating the station for the family's forthcoming Christmas at Sandringham.*

➤ *The coronation of Queen Elizabeth II in 1953 was an excuse for celebrations across the nation. Many stations were decorated. This extravagant display was at Bristol Temple Meads.*

BRITISH RAILWAYS
SOUTHERN REGION

INSTRUCTIONS TO

STATION MASTERS, INSPECTORS, DRIVERS, MOTORMEN, GUARDS, SIGNALMEN, CROSSING KEEPERS, PERMANENT WAY STAFF AND ALL OTHERS CONCERNED

AS TO

A ROYAL SPECIAL TRAIN

CONVEYING

THEIR MAJESTIES

THE KING AND QUEEN

WATERLOO to SHERBORNE

AND

SHERBORNE to WATERLOO

ON

THURSDAY, 1st JUNE, 1950

➤ *Every royal train movement required the preparation of special orders for the day. The instructions were issued to everyone on the route involved in the operation of the train.*

↟ Her Majesty the Queen prepares to leave the royal train at Newton Abbot station, in Devon, on a visit to the Royal Show in the 1950s.

↟ The full royal train includes a dining saloon with full kitchen facilities, as well as carriages for day and night use. Here, during a visit by Princess Elizabeth in the early 1950s, the table in the dining saloon is being laid.

↟ HRH Princess Margaret is greeted at Birmingham International station, on the occasion of a royal visit in January 1979.

Until recently, royal and state visitors were transported on special trains to London from Southampton docks, or later from Gatwick airport. These were usually assembled from Pullmans, though occasionally royal carriages could be attached. These journeys, however short, also required special movement instructions. The train below, three Pullmans headed by Battle of Britain Class No. 34088, '213 Squadron', carried the President of the Cameroons from London Victoria to Gatwick at the end of his state visit in May 1963.

Private—For use of the Staff concerned only.

B.R. 31057
Notice No. 798AGM(T) 1961

BRITISH RAILWAYS
SOUTHERN REGION

NOTICE
OF
PRESIDENTIAL SPECIAL TRAIN
CONVEYING

HIS EXCELLENCY
THE PRESIDENT OF THE
REPUBLIC OF TUNISIA
accompanied by
MADAME BOURGUIBA
and suite

GATWICK AIRPORT TO VICTORIA

TUESDAY, 16th MAY, 1961

This Notice must be acknowledged immediately by use of the enclosed form.

THE BROADS

200 MILES SAFE INLAND WATERWAYS

HOLIDAYS AFLOAT £4 PER WEEK

PARTICULARS OF TRAIN SERVICE, FARES ETC. FROM L·N·E·R INQUIRY OFFICES OR STATIONS. DESCRIPTIVE GUIDE (PRICE 6ᵈ) FROM NORFOLK BROADS BUREAU. BROADLAND HOUSE. NEWGATE STREET. LONDON. E.C.I.

HUNSTANTON

HU

ILLUSTRAT
ASSOCIAT

IN AND AROUND
**EASTERN
ENGLAND**

NSTANTON

T'S QUICKER BY RAIL

GUIDE FROM SECRETARY ADVANCEMENT
N OR ANY L·N·E·R OFFICE OR AGENCY

STATION SCENES

Eastern England's railway map developed steadily from the 1840s, when some of the main lines were built, often by predominantly local companies. A number of these came together in 1862 to form the Great Eastern. Local, cross-country and branch lines were added to the map through the last decades of the 19th century, notably the extensive and largely rural network spread across Norfolk by the Midland & Great Northern Joint Railway. In due course the LNER and then British Railways took over. In the 1960s many of the rural routes were lost as the emphasis switched to the main lines and the expanding commuter traffic. Much of the network and its infrastructure have disappeared, but there are plenty of photographs left that document station life in this part of England.

◁ The LNER used local exhibitions of locomotives and rolling stock to publicize its services and its modern image. Here, in Ilford, Essex, in June 1934, a gaggle of schoolboys wait to board the footplate of an industrial locomotive.

▽ British Railways was keen to underline its new and modern look during the early 1960s. One of several new stations built at this time was Barking, in Essex, seen here in a 1961 publicity photograph that highlights its predominantly concrete construction.

◁ Hadham, seen here in May 1957, was an intermediate station on the Buntingford branch, which had opened in 1863. The scene, as the driver waits to take the single-line token, is quite traditional, with an old bench and platform lights, but the nameboard shows that some modernization had taken place. The line closed in 1965.

▽ A busy 1960s scene at Abbey Wood, a Thames-side commuter line. The crossing gates are opening and a throng of passengers from the departing train push forward. On the other side, a Ford Anglia and a woman with a smart pram wait more patiently.

▽ A young, neatly dressed enthusiast poses for a friend on the platform at Beckton in the 1950s. Even then this was a remote East London location, the last passenger station on a line built primarily to serve the Beckton gas works – visible in the distance beyond the rather ramshackle timber station buildings.

△ This view of Henham Halt, a minor station on the Thaxted branch in Essex, shows the delightfully primitive nature of some rural stations. An elderly carriage body, an old bench and a lamp were deemed sufficient for passenger needs on a line that closed as early as 1952.

▽ The Essex branch from Wivenhoe to Brightlingsea closed in 1964. Here, shortly before closure, a DMU waits quietly in the platform for passengers who probably will not appear. It is a scene typical of many a rural branch line at this time. The line opened in 1866 for fish traffic, particularly oysters.

Cambridge Station

△ This Edwardian postcard shows Cambridge's famously long main platform, which was built to serve trains in both directions. Staff pose for the camera as the Great Eastern Railway's London-bound express pulls in.

▷ It is a busy morning in the mid-1950s at Dunmow, on the line from Bishop's Stortford to Braintree & Bocking, as passengers prepare to join an excursion to Clacton for a day at the seaside. This line, which had opened in 1869 after a long building period, lost its passenger service in 1952 and was then used only occasionally for excursions.

▽ As a railwayman cycles towards the station to take up his duties on a sunny day in March 1959, an express leaves Colchester, hauled by an LNER B1 Class locomotive, No. 61279.

▷ The locomotive and the rolling stock suggest this could be a scene from the 1930s or earlier. In fact, it is Ipswich in the mid-1950s, with a London-bound train from Yarmouth in the platform.

▽ Halesworth, Suffolk, was famous for the 1888 movable platform extensions incorporating the level crossing. Here, in the 1950s, enthusiasts of all ages take a good look.

◁ Lowestoft Central was a grand station, built progressively from 1847 and a reflection of the way the railway created this popular resort. This Edwardian view shows it in its heyday.

▽ The branch to Mildenhall from Cambridge closed in 1962. Here, shortly before closure, a small boy in a slightly oversize coat walks down the deserted platform towards the waiting DMU.

◁ Wighton Halt, south of Wells-next-the-Sea in north Norfolk, was a typical rural station with nothing but a corrugated iron passenger shed, a lamp and an overgrown flower bed to its name. In June 1963 it was deserted except for a bicycle, which probably belonged to the photographer. The line closed the following year.

▷ Cromer High, opened in 1877, was the town's first station, but it was the better-placed Cromer Beach station, opened ten years later, that really made the town into a resort. Cromer High closed in 1954, and this shows the substantial station in a state of dereliction in 1964, shortly before demolition.

▽ Wisbech North, one of three stations with Wisbech in their name, was built as part of the Midland & Great Northern's network. After final closure in 1965, the buildings lingered on and were used for a while as a garage.

ALONG HOLIDAY LINES

East Anglia, with its combination of easily accessible countryside, seaside resorts and historic towns and villages, has always appealed to holidaymakers, and the railways were quick to exploit this. From early days, companies offered a wide variety of day excursions from major London stations, notably Liverpool Street, Kings Cross and Fenchurch Street, and this pattern was maintained to the end of the British Rail era. Also popular were the coastal towns of Essex, Suffolk and Norfolk, the majority of which were connected to the surprisingly extensive rural railway network that covered the map of East Anglia until the 1960s. Another well-known holiday area was the Norfolk Broads, which was equally well served.

▽ ▷ Day trips and weekly holiday and Runabout tickets were extensively marketed from the 1900s, with some typically stylish publicity brochures in the 1930s and 1950s. Some of these tickets included stations serving the Broads, where many visitors enjoyed the experience of exploring the waterways in wherry-type yachts.

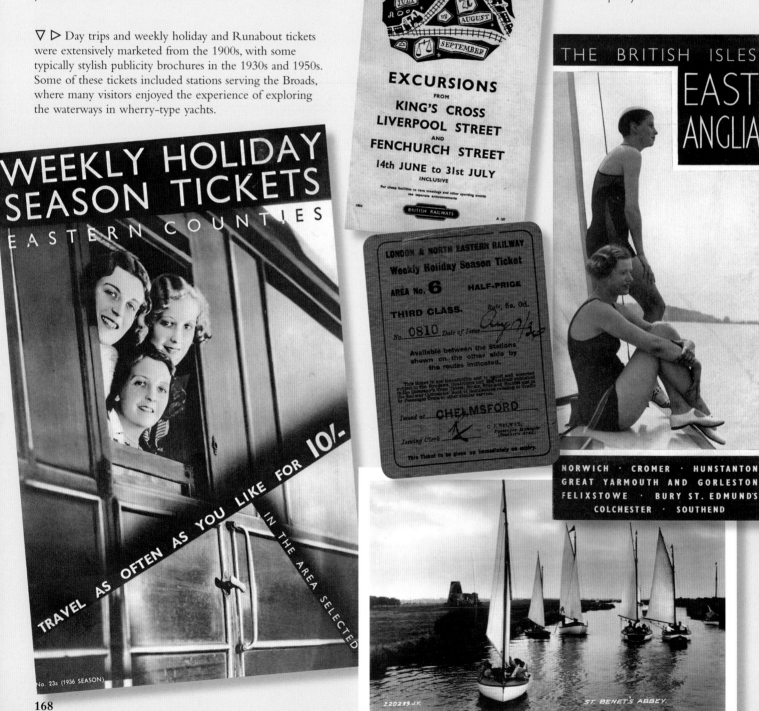

ESSEX

BRITISH RAILWAYS

"Off the beaten track on the Great Eastern"

The Sudbury Branch: Walks 5-8
Valid until 31 December 1993

Network SouthEast

RAMBLES IN
EPPING FOREST

BRITISH RAILWAYS

1/-

△ ▽ ▷ The accessibility of good walking country in Essex was something the railways made the most of, as these brochures and booklets from the 1950s and the 1990s demonstrate. The photograph below shows LNER locomotives at Stratford depot being prepared for holiday traffic which, at the August peak, could total over a hundred holiday and excursion trains per day.

READY FOR THE HOLIDAYS

DISCOVER
East Suffolk
on Britain's Scenic Railway

GREAT EASTERN

A.100X (HD)

COMBINED RAIL AND RIVER TRIPS
TO
IPSWICH
AND
HARWICH
or vice versa
THURSDAYS
12th JUNE to 11th SEPTEMBER

Rail to Harwich
Steamer Harwich to Ipswich
Rail from Ipswich

This tour can also be made in the reverse direction

From	Return fare (second class rail)
ROMFORD	11/9d.
CHELMSFORD	9/6d.
COLCHESTER	6/3d.
MANNINGTREE	5/6d.

Children 3 years of age and under 14, slightly above half-fares

A most interesting cruise on the River Orwell including a view of shipping in Harwich Harbour, Trinity House vessels and H.M.S. Ganges (Boys' Naval Training Establishment) and the famous Pin Mill

Light refreshments and tea obtainable on board the motor vessel. Fully Licensed bar

See over for details of rail services and boat times

Tickets can be obtained IN ADVANCE at stations and travel agencies

Further information will be supplied on application to stations, offices, travel agencies or to Traffic Manager, Hamilton House, Bishopsgate, London, E.C.2 (Tel : Bishopsgate 2600) ; or District Commercial Officer, Ipswich (Tel : Ipswich 4375)

London, April 1958

SOUTHEND
ON SEA
Westcliff   Leigh
Thorpe Bay
Shoeburyness
Playground of the South

PLEASE RETAIN THIS BILL FOR REFERENCE

A620/R(H.D.)

SUNDAY, 22nd AUGUST, 1954
SEASIDE EXCURSION
(With BUFFET FACILITIES)
TO
YARMOUTH
(VAUXHALL)

FROM	TIMES OF DEPARTURE	RETURN FARES (Third Class)	ARRIVAL TIMES ON RETURN
NOTTINGHAM (Midland)	a.m. 8 35 9 35	16/0	p.m. 12 30
STAMFORD TOWN	10 54	14/0	p.m. 11 22
YARMOUTH (Vauxhall) arrive	p.m. 1 14		depart 5 0

FOR DETAILS OF LATE 'BUSES AT NOTTINGHAM—see over

Travel in Rail Comfort

BRITISH RAILWAYS

BRITISH RAILWAYS

A 77 (e) HD

HOLIDAY PRE-VIEW EXCURSION
An opportunity to see and book your holiday accommodation
FELIXSTOWE
SUNDAY 29th APRIL

OUTWARD JOURNEY		Return fares third class	RETURN JOURNEY (same day only)	
London (Liverpool Street)	a.m. dep. 9 20	s. d.	Felixstowe (Town)	dep. p.m. 7 30
Ilford	—		Colchester	arr. 8 43
Romford	9 40		Chelmsford	9 11
Shenfield	9 50	10/4	Shenfield	9 22
Chelmsford	10 3	10/4	Romford	9 27
Colchester	10 25	9/-	Ilford	9 41
	10 55	5/-	London (Liverpool Street)	9 51
Felixstowe (Town)	arr. p.m. 12 4			10 7

Buffet facilities will be available on the train in both directions

HOSTESSES FROM THE FELIXSTOWE PUBLICITY AND ADVANCEMENT ASSOCIATION WILL TRAVEL ON THE TRAIN FROM LIVERPOOL STREET AND WILL BE PLEASED TO SUPPLY LITERATURE AND INFORMATION ON THE HOLIDAY AMENITIES OFFERED

For other bookings in connection with this excursion, see separate handbill

Tickets can be obtained IN ADVANCE at stations, offices and travel agencies

For further information apply to L. I. Moorcock, London, E.C.2 (Tel : Bishopsgate 7600, Extn. 2358) ; R. S. Lawler, Ipswich (Tel : Ipswich 4375) ; or to B. X Jerrow, Commercial Manager, Liverpool Street station, London, E.C.2 (Tel : Bishopsgate 7600)

CONDITIONS OF ISSUE

Conditions applicable to British Railways exhibited in their excursion or circulated free of charge at stations

LUGGAGE ALLOWANCES are as set out in these general notices

Children under three years of age, free ; three years and under fourteen, half-fare

London, April 1956

Published by British Railways (Eastern Region)   Printed in Great Britain

Railway publicity has always promoted regions, resorts and particular holiday and excursion destinations, and many trains brought visitors to East Anglia from well outside the region. Holidaymakers, of course, sent postcards home: this one, of Great Yarmouth, dates from 1910.

Great Yarmouth. Wellington Pier and Gardens.

CRUISING ON THE NORFOLK BROADLANDS

Beach and Pier, Hunstanton.

◁ ▽ Cruising on the Broads or enjoying the beach at Hunstanton were timeless pleasures, the latter's popularity being based partly on the pier and the sands, and partly on its proximity to Sandringham. For the railways, the family was always important, and publicity was often family-orientated, as in this 1966 example.

British Rail | Eastern Region

RED FOLDER

Fenchurch Street, Leyton, Barking & Tilbury Area

BARGAIN OFFERS

FOR 1966

Folder No. 14

▽ Several preserved railways operate successfully in East Anglia, but an important pioneer was the Bressingham Steam Museum in Norfolk, with its collection of locomotives of many gauges and sizes. Here, visitors ride behind a 1909 Hunslet narrow gauge quarry locomotive from Penrhyn.

No. 994

ALONG PRESERVED LINES

The North Norfolk Railway, generally known as the Poppy Line, operates along a section of the old Midland & Great Northern Joint Railway between Holt and Sheringham, where there is a connection with the national rail network. Besides the usual mix of timetabled services and special events, the railway has a dedicated education centre, offering dramatic indoor and out-of-classroom activities and field trips for parties of up to 70 children. The programme is structured to support National Curriculum key stages, and the railway has been awarded the government's Learning outside the Classroom Quality Mark. Themed days include 'The Evacuee Experience in World War II', and 'Aunt Dotty's Seaside Adventure'.

▷ Always popular is the dramatic re-creation of the experience of children being sent as evacuees away from their homes and families during the dark days of 1940. Here, children, in period dress and complete with gas masks, are being escorted onto a train for a journey to an unknown destination and an uncertain future, in which ration books and air raid precautions will play a major part.

ESCAPE FROM SCHOOL!
Enjoy out-of-classroom education on the Poppy Line
Visit www.poppylineeducation.com

POPPY LINE
NORTH NORFOLK RAILWAY

World War 2 – The Evacuees • The Rhyme & Rhythm of the Railway
• Aunty Dotty's Seaside Adventure • Spy School • A Victorian Journey • Science Days

When the education centre was formally opened, the celebration had a Victorian theme, looking back to the opening of the railway in 1887. This theme is now structured as a Victorian train journey, on which the children are taken to a new workhouse in order to escape an outbreak of scarlet fever.

NORTH NORFOLK RAILWAY
Sheringham Station
PLATFORM TICKET
Available One Hour
Not Transferable   No Public Liability

▷ The operation of the railway is not part of the Education Centre's events and activities, but there are occasions when children can be shown parts of the railway's infrastructure, including the signal box.

▽ With unfamiliar formality, children line up to board the evacuees' special train.

R.C.T.S.
THE
FENSMAN

65562

SPECIALS & TOURS

Railway enthusiasts have always existed, fascinated by the trains and their history, the engineering and the running of the railways. The Victorians were keen amateur timekeepers, publishing their findings in specialist magazines, which became popular in the late 1800s. These, and the many railway societies, began to run enthusiasts' specials, visiting little-known parts of the network or tracking down ancient locomotives and rolling stock. With closure programmes and the impending demise of steam in the mid-20th century, these specials – which often provided printed itineraries and souvenir tickets – grew in popularity. The railtour is still important in the world of the enthusiast, particularly as modern regulations limit individual exploration.

◀ In the past it was much easier for enthusiasts to arrange private visits. Here, in September 1964, three young men, armed with notebooks and a camera, have made their way into Nine Elms depot. Two have posed with Battle of Britain Class No. 34051, 'Sir Winston Churchill', which was being prepared for the day's work. In January 1965 this locomotive would head Sir Winston's funeral train.

➤ On a sunny day an enthusiast sits on the grassy bank outside Dainton tunnel in Somerset, watching a Western Class diesel storm out in a cloud of smoke. He is holding his camera, but not taking a photograph – perhaps more concerned with his pose for his friend's picture.

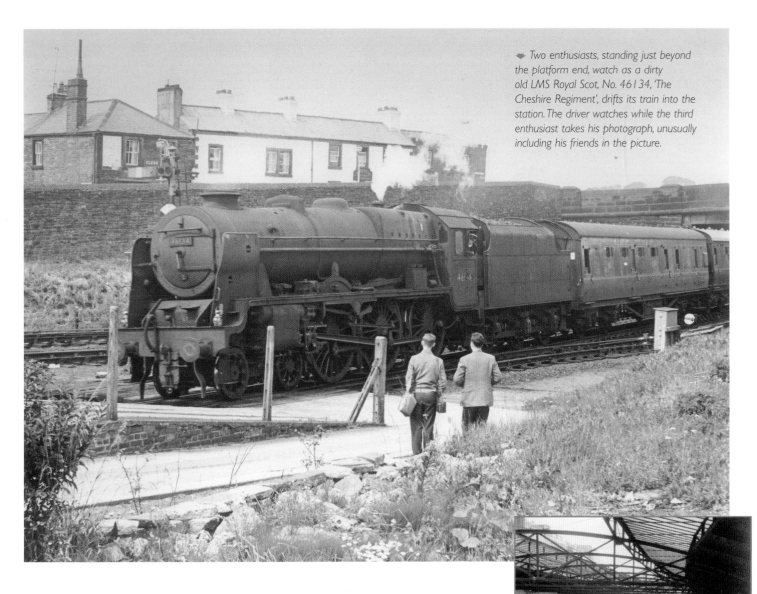

Two enthusiasts, standing just beyond the platform end, watch as a dirty old LMS Royal Scot, No. 46134, 'The Cheshire Regiment', drifts its train into the station. The driver watches while the third enthusiast takes his photograph, unusually including his friends in the picture.

This group, of mixed ages but all wearing or carrying regulation mackintoshes, are members of the Bristol Railway Circle on an organized visit to Avonmouth Dock shed in June 1954. They are posing in front of 'Hallen', a Port of Bristol Authority Peckett locomotive of 1943.

London Transport continued to use steam on maintenance trains until 1972. In that year there were a number of farewell performances by the last steam locomotives. This demonstration by L9 was for the crowds at Farringdon station.

Manchester University Railway Society
THE STAFFORDSHIRE POTTER
13th MARCH, 1965
Route: Ancoats, Stockport, Northwich,
Stoke, Congleton, Cauldon Quarry,
Stoke, Bollington, Ancoats.
FOR CONDITIONS SEE ITINERARY
NOT TRANSFERABLE
Williamson, Ticket Printer, Ashton-u-Lyne
0960

☛ *Passenger traffic ceased on the branch to Abingdon, also in Oxfordshire, in 1963, but the line remained open for the car factory until 1984, so a number of specials visited it. Here, in the late 1960s, a DMU disgorges its crowd of enthusiasts onto the closed platforms.*

☛ *Looking rather cheerful, perhaps because of the presence of so many women, these enthusiasts are taking part in the last day events on the Woodstock branch, Oxfordshire, in 1954.*

THE
RAILWAY CORRESPONDENCE AND
TRAVEL SOCIETY

—

ITINERARY
OF THE
NORTH EAST LONDON
RAIL TOUR
29th MARCH, 1952

☛ *An unusual visitor to Epsom Downs station in the mid-1960s was 'The Surrey Rambler' railtour, headed by a smart-looking rebuilt Battle of Britain Class locomotive, No. 34089, '602 Squadron'. The passengers, milling about on the platform of this terminus station, include a number of families and children making the most of a day out.*

On a wet day in October 1960 the Midland & Great Northern Society Waveney Valley special pauses at Reepham station in Norfolk. The enthusiasts have scattered to take their photographs.

SOUTHERN COUNTIES TOURING SOCIETY
(Founded 1947)

RAILWAY TOURS SECTION

ITINERARY
of the
"The Southern Wanderer"

VICTORIA (Central)		CRYSTAL PALACE
WALLINGTON	DORKING	HORSHAM
SOUTHAMPTON	TEMPLECOMBE	SALISBURY
EAST PUTNEY		VICTORIA (Eastern)

SUNDAY, 28th MARCH, 1965

PRICE 2/6

Built for the London, Tilbury & Southend Railway in 1909, the 4-4-2 passenger locomotive 'Thundersley' was finally withdrawn in 1956 and subsequently preserved for the National Rail Collection. On a wet day in March 1956 the locomotive waits to haul a farewell enthusiasts' special from Southend.

Many enthusiasts' societies liked to combine their railtours with the use of unusual rolling stock. In the 1950s, a group has travelled along a branch closed to passengers in 1951 to Faringdon, Oxfordshire, in an old GWR railcar.

In 1955 members of the Loughborough Railway Society pose in a brake van during their visit to Loughborough Derby Road station. The group includes the inspector, the guard and the fireman, as well as Mrs Millie Mason, who seems to be enjoying herself, and the young Master Newton.

In extreme conditions, some of the group who have travelled to Loch Tay, the old terminus of a branch from Killin Junction, have left the train to take their photographs. Passenger services between Killin and Loch Tay station ceased in 1939, but the line survived until services between Killin Junction and Killin ceased in 1965.

The Railway Correspondence and Travel Society has been in existence for over 75 years and is still one of the leading enthusiasts' groups, organizing a full programme of tours and visits every year. This photograph shows members visiting Severn Beach station in June 1995, having travelled there in a Class 143 DMU in Regional Railways livery.

BRITISH RAILWAYS (S)
RAILWAY CORRESPONDENCE
& TRAVEL SOCIETY
BRIGHTON WORKS CENTENARY
Available on DAY of issue ONLY.
Pullman Special
VICTORIA to BRIGHTON & Return
also Special Train
BRIGHTON to KEMP TOWN (Goods)
& Return
THIRD CLASS 5th. OCTOBER 1952
FOR CONDITIONS SEE BACK.
0250

➥ The running of steam-hauled specials on the main line has been popular since they were re-introduced in the late 1970s, and there is now an ambitious annual programme. Many enthusiasts travel on them – but far more gather along the route to watch.

➥ The flourishing railway preservation movement has made it easier for enthusiasts to pursue their passions. Here, in the 1970s, a group poses in front of 'Lydham Manor', prior to taking their double-headed train along the Paignton & Dartmouth Steam Railway from Kingswear. This heritage line opened in 1973.

MAN & MACHINE

Thousands of people lined up to see Stephenson's 'Rocket', and it is likely that most of them were men. This was the start of an enduring relationship between railways, and locomotives in particular, and the male species. It is not a matter of age. Small boys and old men stand and stare, and many become fascinated by the history, the technical details and the individual quirks of these machines. Steam has an understandable magic, but men will look at any locomotive and almost any kind of train. There is a huge library that documents this relationship, one that often started with toys and was then further developed by models. Most men want to drive locomotives and, in extreme cases, some end up owning one.

➦ In September 1960 an LMS Patriot Class locomotive waits at Carlisle station, at the head of a stopping train to Maryport and Whitehaven. Small boys wait around, notebooks in hand, but it is the man that stands out. Hatted, with a belted mackintosh and a classic briefcase, he looks straight at the photographer. However, it is the locomotive that has drawn him to the end of the platform, far away from the train he presumably has to catch.

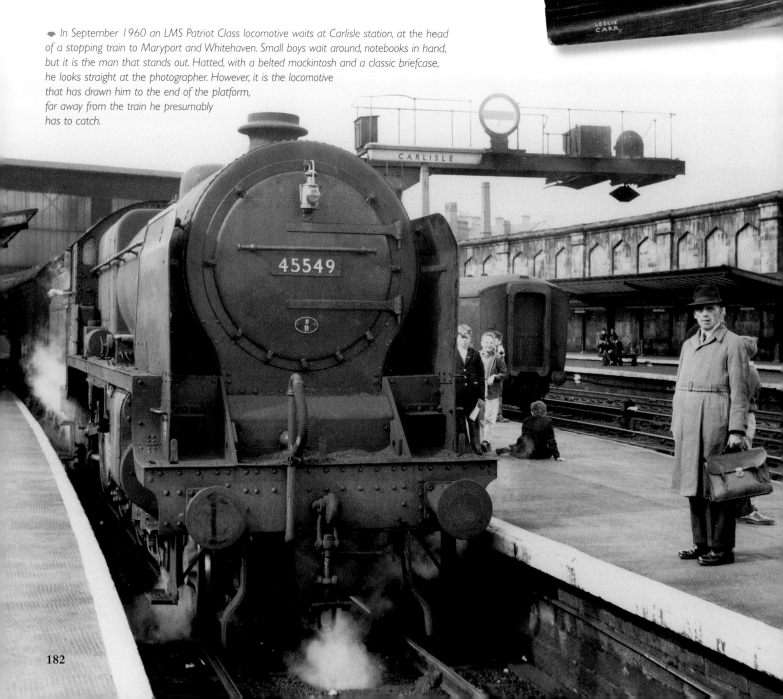

All locomotives are interesting, but some seem to evoke unusual enthusiasm and a devoted following. A classic example is the group of Pacific locomotives developed by Oliver Bulleid for the Southern Railway from 1941, memorable for their advanced mechanics and air-smoothed casing. In all, there were 140 locomotives in three classes, Battle of Britain, West Country and Merchant Navy. This 1947 card of 'Sidmouth' highlights the sense of speed and style.

Till death us do part: one man's personal passion for Battle of Britain Class 34081, '92 Squadron', is permanently marked by a tattoo.

For many, the chance to see and photograph a steam locomotive is not to be missed. This man, sporting his 1970s flares and tight jumper, has made his way across a derelict industrial landscape in northern England to find the best position to capture a passing enthusiasts' special.

The appeal of the Bulleid Pacific was immediate. They looked and sounded different. This young man has wheeled his bike to the far end of the platform to get a good look at 'Barnstaple', an early West Country Class locomotive, which stands ready to draw its long train out of the station. It is the late 1940s, in the early days of British Railways. 'Barnstaple' is still in Southern colours, but has its BR number.

🔺 *There can be no clearer example of the special relationship between man and machine: the man – middle-aged, suited, standing at ease, savouring the moment; the machine – an LMS Jubilee, No. 45733, 'Novelty', shrouded in steam and ready to depart from some large station in the North or the Midlands in the late 1950s. The driver looks on, impassive.*

▶ *An elderly enthusiast has gone as far as the platform slope at Oxford to get a good view, and he has been rewarded as GWR Castle Class No. 4093, 'Dunster Castle', backs out of the station. Meanwhile an unusual visitor from the South, West Country Class No. 34103, 'Calstock', waits at the head of a Bournemouth-to-Kidsgrove holiday express. It is a wet September day in 1965 and steam is on its way out. 'Calstock' has already lost the crest below the nameplate.*

The subterranean gloom of Birmingham New Street has been enlivened by the sight of another locomotive class popular with enthusiasts, a Class 50 diesel. Here, in May 1981, No. 50039, 'Implacable', waits at the head of a Paddington train. The young man, standing as close as he can, is either lost in admiration or is in conversation with the driver. The locomotive seems to have been freshly painted in the BR livery of that era.

In August 1951 the Saint Mungo express stands in Perth station, ready to depart for Glasgow. At its head is a smart British Railways Standard Class locomotive, No. 73009. As this type was introduced in that year, this locomotive must be almost brand new. No doubt that is the subject of the conversation taking place between the driver and the gentleman who has made his way to the far end of the platform, umbrella in hand, for that special enthusiast's moment.

RAILWAY CHILDREN

By the end of the 19th century railway enthusiasts were being actively encouraged by the publication of a number of specialist books and magazines – though often discouraged by the railway companies. By the 1920s the numbering and naming of locomotives was being standardized, and trainspotting (a term that was not actually in use until the 1950s) developed as a national pastime, particularly among children. Cigarette cards and published lists of locomotives were a further encouragement, and from the 1950s onwards the sight of small boys, equipped with notebooks, pencils and, occasionally, cameras, had become a perennial feature on station platforms everywhere.

In this classic image, a small boy in school uniform, alone on the platform of Birmingham New Street sometime in the 1950s, captures in his notebook an LMS Jubilee No. 45651, 'Shovell' (from a group named after admirals). From the cab, the fireman watches him.

Although some railway companies published lists of their locomotives, it was effectively the Ian Allan 'ABC' series that made trainspotting a universal pastime. Launched during World War II, the series has since been greatly expanded.

Another small boy in his school uniform and another Jubilee, this time No. 45738, 'Samson'. This is Birmingham New Street during the 1950s, and the London-to-Wolverhampton express is about to depart – but not before the locomotive has been spotted and noted.

Trainspotters traditionally love steam, but diesels too have their own kind of appeal. Here, in the 1960s, two boys watch closely as the DMU from Maiden Newton drifts into the platform at Bridport, Dorset, the end of the branch. The station nameboard says Bridport for West Bay, the former terminus of the line a couple of miles further on.

A diesel-hauled train pauses at Lidlington, on the Bletchley-to-Bedford line, while several enthusiasts look on. Two of them are writing in their notebooks, while two others watch the photographer. The boy in the foreground, who seems to be outgrowing his trousers, has not bothered to get his camera out.

187

♦ Trainspotting has no limits, and a locomotive on a miniature line can be exciting. Here, in the 1930s, two small boys seem fascinated both by a large Bassett-Lowke engine and the photographer. The adult enthusiast, wearing his tie outside his tightly buttoned jacket, seems a bit uncertain.

♦ Casually seated on an old brick wall, a small boy enjoys his moment with an ex-LNER Class V2 locomotive outside a shed in the north of Britain. Today, such a close encounter between boy and machine is inconceivable.

♦ Another young boy concentrates on capturing on film a busy moment on the Ravenglass & Eskdale Light Railway in Cumbria, while the driver of 'River Esk' gestures – rather strangely – with his shovel.

♦ With his hands in his pockets and his socks round his ankles, this young enthusiast is making the most of his luck as Class 9F No. 92220, 'Evening Star', the last steam locomotive built by British Railways, pauses at Templecombe in the mid-1960s while in charge of a holiday express on the Somerset & Dorset route.

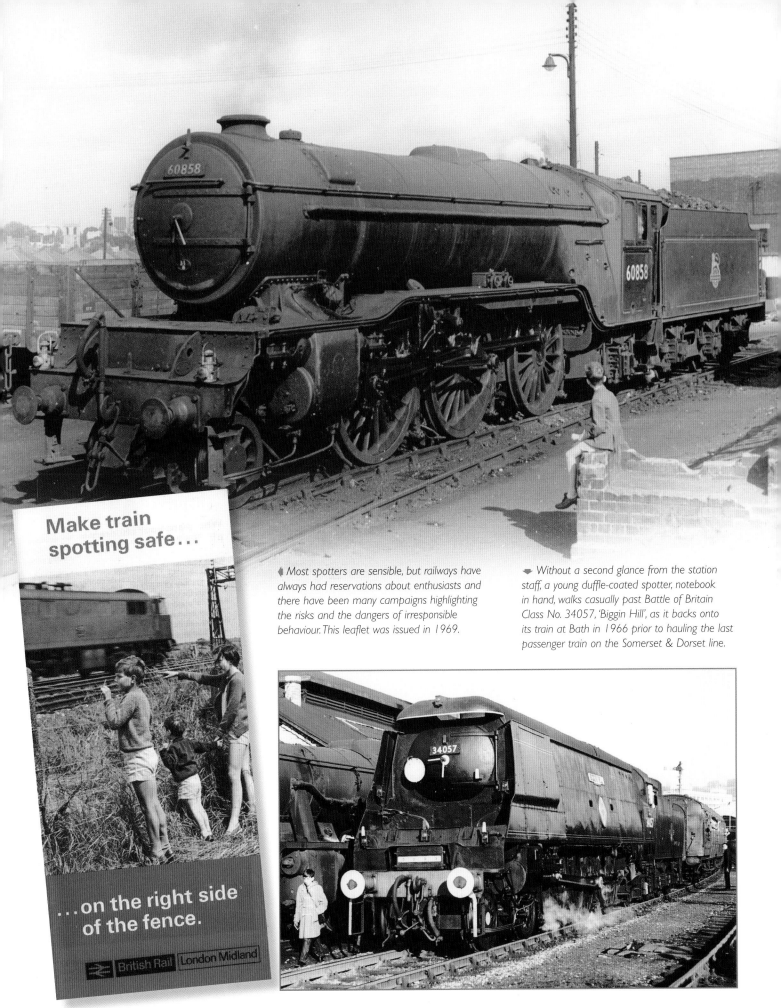

Most spotters are sensible, but railways have always had reservations about enthusiasts and there have been many campaigns highlighting the risks and the dangers of irresponsible behaviour. This leaflet was issued in 1969.

Without a second glance from the station staff, a young duffle-coated spotter, notebook in hand, walks casually past Battle of Britain Class No. 34057, 'Biggin Hill', as it backs onto its train at Bath in 1966 prior to hauling the last passenger train on the Somerset & Dorset line.

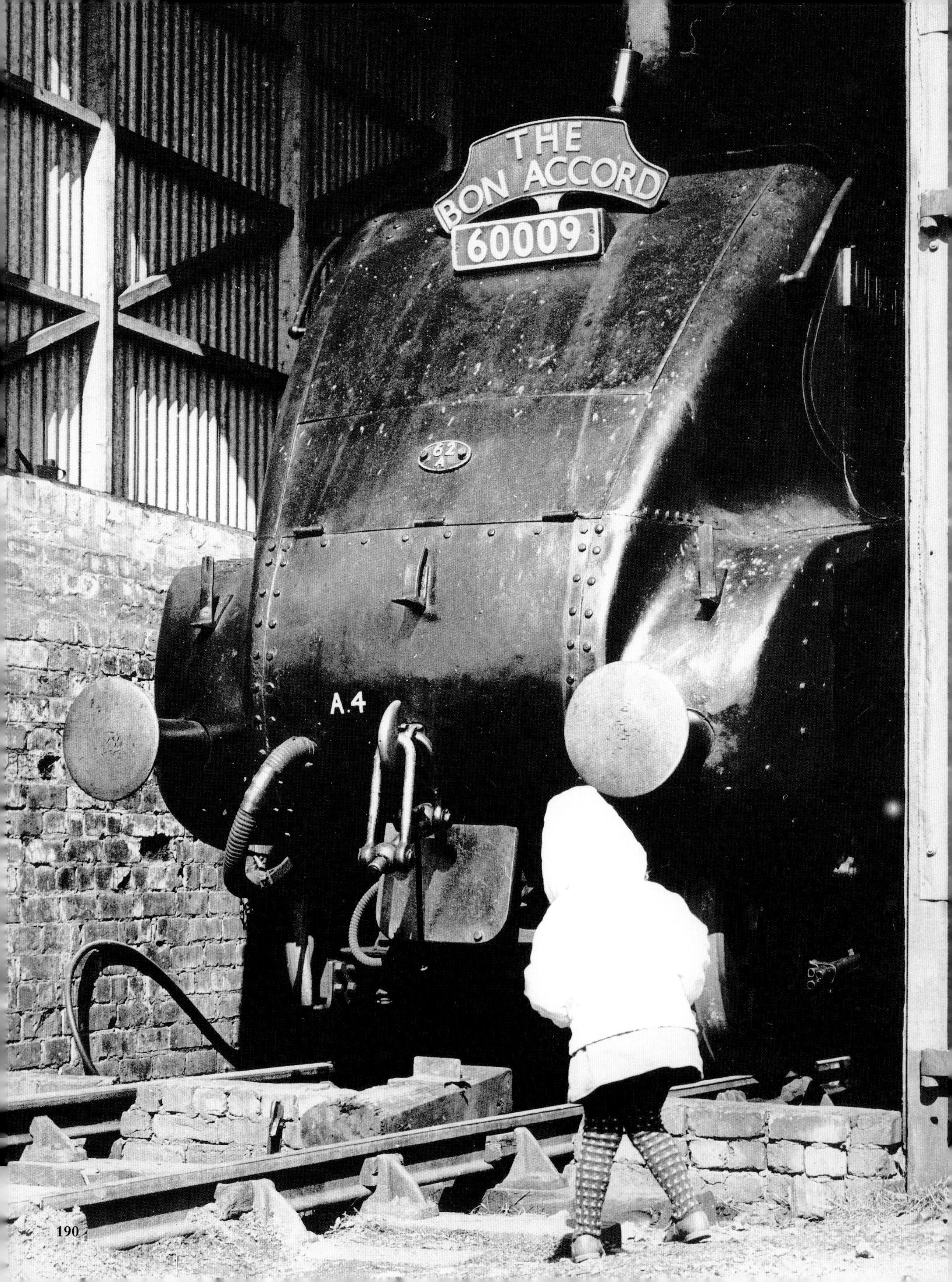
THE
BON ACCORD
60009
62
A
A.4

◀ This young boy, typically in his school uniform, cannot believe his luck as he has the rare chance to explore the smokebox of a brand new LNER locomotive, while the photographer grabs the chance of an unusual publicity shot.

◀ It's never too soon to start being a trainspotter. This little girl, apparently fearless, comes face to face with the streamlined nose of the famous preserved Gresley A4, No. 60009, 'Union of South Africa'.

▶ A small child drags on his mother's arm, perhaps overcome by the sight and sound of a Bristol-to-Paddington express on the approach to Box tunnel, Wiltshire, in the summer of 1964.

◆ Another spotter in the making sits in his pushchair watching intently as Deltic 9017, 'The Durham Light Infantry', hauls the up Flying Scotsman past Wylam, Northumbria, on 24 July 1972. The train was on a diversionary route because of engineering work near Dunbar.

☛ While his father reads his book with his back to the action, a young enthusiast leans out over the platform at Honiton, in Devon, to see the approaching Penzance-to-Paddington train hauled by a Class 52 diesel, 'Western Chieftain'. Meanwhile, the Leeds-to-Penzance train passes through the station. He probably knew that, because of diversions in April 1974, these were unusual sights.

☛ Two young children, one in a pram, watch closely as an elderly Manning Wardle tank locomotive, perhaps No. 5 of 1919, hauls its train slowly along a street on the route of the Weston-super-Mare, Clevedon & Portishead Railway. The date is probably the 1930s, when this rather eccentric 14-mile line was operated by the famous Colonel Stephens.

◗ The links between children and the railways went beyond trainspotting. Many children's books and comics featured railway stories and train journeys, and there were a number of postcards inspired by the idea of children travelling on their own and the problems that happened en route. Children regularly travelled unaccompanied, usually in the care of the guard, but even so there must have been crises caused by lost tickets or mislaid luggage. This Edwardian card, carefully posed on a real station, turns the incident of the lost ticket into a major drama.

6757 A   "THE LOST TICKET."

ROTARY PHOTO. E.C.

London & South Western Railway Servant's Orphanage. BOYS GYMNASTIC SET PIECE.

◖ From quite an early date, some railway companies operated their own hospitals and convalescent homes, or were involved in other ways in caring for their workers in times of difficulty. A major concern was the care of children of employees killed on duty. The Midland opened the first railway orphanage in 1875 and the LSWR followed ten years later with theirs. In 1904 this was moved to large and impressive premises beside the main line near Woking, in Surrey. A number of postcards were issued, including this example, to illustrate the activities of the orphanage.

◗ Some trainspotters move on to other things; some develop into lifelong railway enthusiasts. One of the latter wrote a caption for this photograph: 'The sophisticated lass appears not to share the excitement of the young as a Hymeck appears on a St Anne's Board Mill wood pulp train from Portishead at Victoria Park, Bristol, in September 1972.'

HARROGATE

BRITAIN'S 100% SPA

ILLUSTRATED BROCHURE free on application to any G.N.R. Office or Superintendent of the Line, King's Cross Station, London, N.1.

GRE

FOR PA
AND OT
GREAT

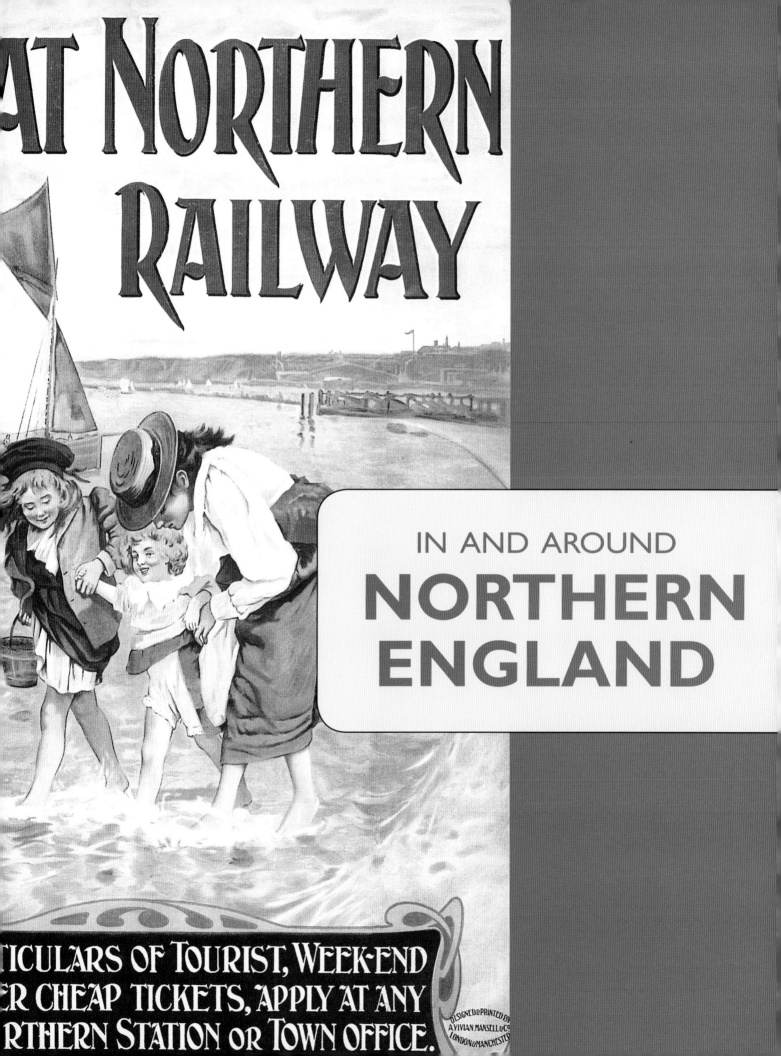

STATION SCENES

The North of England has long been blessed by a remarkable range of stations, from big city termini to remote country halts. It was here that the railways were invented and developed, so the habit of going to stations and taking, or watching, trains was instilled early in the minds of a curious public. As elsewhere, the images selected indicate the endless diversity of the photographer's imagination and vision. Some photographers like crowded scenes, some emptiness, some pick the special occasion, and some give the impression that they just happened to be passing. What unites them is their love of railways, and their legacy is a mixture of the familiar and the unfamiliar, the scenes still to be enjoyed and those lost for ever.

▽ A rare moment, captured on 1 July 1983, when British Rail's experimental Advanced Passenger Train made a visit to Manchester Piccadilly: the train is ready to leave the almost empty platform, and the guard is a blur of activity.

▷ Manchester Central is lost as a city terminus, though the main building survives as an exhibition centre. It seems unusually quiet in this postcard view, but its importance early in the 20th century is clear.

CENTRAL STATION, MANCHESTER.

InterCity APT

370 006

△ Southport Chapel Street was, in 1958, one of at least seven stations either serving the town or having 'Southport' incorporated in its name. Prior to the departure of the 09.55 to Manchester on a cold December morning, stationmaster and driver confer – once a common event to be witnessed at big stations everywhere.

△ The British Railways photographer must have waited a long time at Carlisle to pick a moment, probably in the 1960s, when nothing was happening and the platforms were largely deserted, at 11.18.

◁ It is a summer's day at York in 1973 and there are plenty of people awaiting the London train. In the foreground a girl with fashionable wedge heels checks her luggage. Over on the opposite platform the Cardiff train is about to depart.

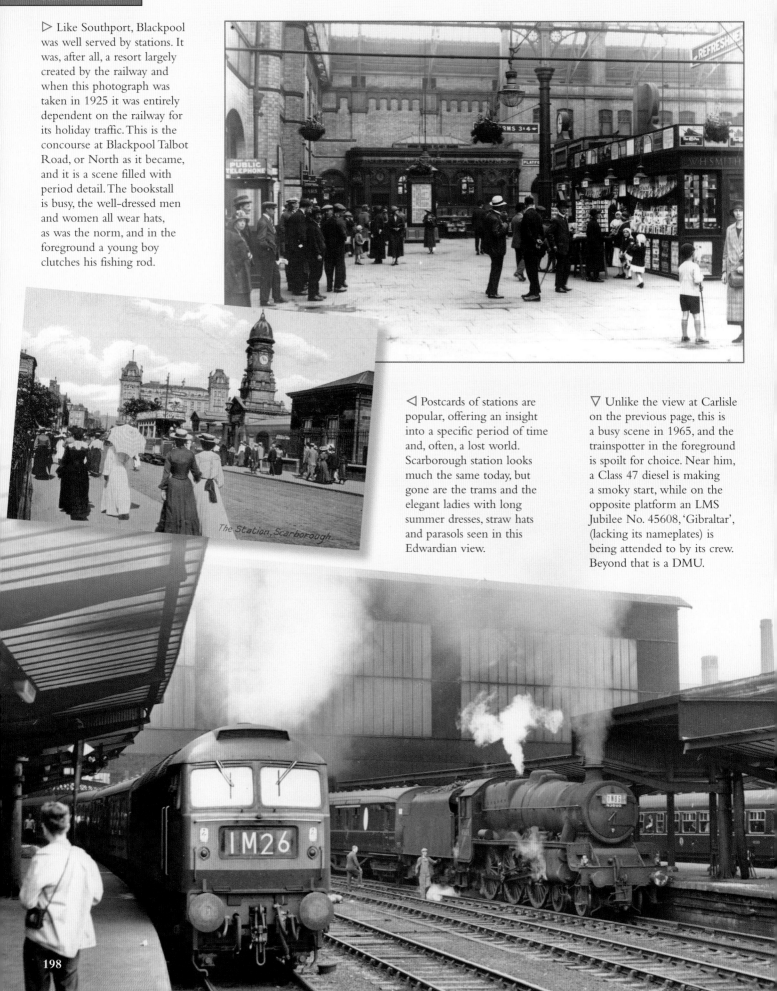

▷ Like Southport, Blackpool was well served by stations. It was, after all, a resort largely created by the railway and when this photograph was taken in 1925 it was entirely dependent on the railway for its holiday traffic. This is the concourse at Blackpool Talbot Road, or North as it became, and it is a scene filled with period detail. The bookstall is busy, the well-dressed men and women all wear hats, as was the norm, and in the foreground a young boy clutches his fishing rod.

The Station, Scarborough

◁ Postcards of stations are popular, offering an insight into a specific period of time and, often, a lost world. Scarborough station looks much the same today, but gone are the trams and the elegant ladies with long summer dresses, straw hats and parasols seen in this Edwardian view.

▽ Unlike the view at Carlisle on the previous page, this is a busy scene in 1965, and the trainspotter in the foreground is spoilt for choice. Near him, a Class 47 diesel is making a smoky start, while on the opposite platform an LMS Jubilee No. 45608, 'Gibraltar', (lacking its nameplates) is being attended to by its crew. Beyond that is a DMU.

△ Most seats are taken in the waiting room at Darlington in this 1973 view, taken by a British Rail photographer who perhaps had time on his hands. Everyone sits well wrapped up, clearly resigned to waiting for some time. The girl with the newspaper is reading about Richard Nixon's visit to Disneyland.

△ This LNWR Official Card shows a busy scene at Liverpool's Riverside station, which was built to serve the North Atlantic liners. This American special to Euston is taking on passengers who have just arrived on one of the great ships of the time, perhaps the *Olympic* or *Mauretania*.

▷ Middlesbrough had a magnificent Gothic station, as seen on this Edwardian card. Completed in 1877, it was one of the town's best buildings. It survives, albeit somewhat reduced in scale by German bombing in World War II.

△ Railways were often affected by floods, and photographs showing the tracks between the platforms turning into a river are not unusual. This is at Cullercoats, near Tynemouth, probably early in the 20th century. Two men gaze gloomily at the photographer, one holding a shunter's pole he has used to check the water's depth.

▽ It is May 1974 and assorted passengers move across the platform at Penrith station, ready to board the London train that is pulling in, hauled by a Class 86 electric locomotive. In the distance a porter, in those days still a regular member of the station staff, struggles with two heavy suitcases.

Something has drawn plenty of people to the platform at Blackburn on a sunny day in the 1960s. Many seem to be mothers with their children, casually dressed and clearly waiting for a particular train to arrive or for something to happen. Among them are a few passengers whose more formal dress reflects the normal life of the station.

▽ A Ford pulls away from a deserted-looking Ashton Charlestown station on a quiet day in the early 1960s. Sited near Stalybridge on a complex tangle of lines northwest of Manchester, the station, built in two-tone brick, was originally part of the Lancashire & Yorkshire network.

▷ Workington, now a rather battered station on the scenic Cumbrian Coast line, was, until 1966, the terminus of the line from Penrith across the Lake District via Keswick. This postcard view, with its curiously random scattering of people, shows the station in its better days.

STATION APPROACH, WORKINGTON.

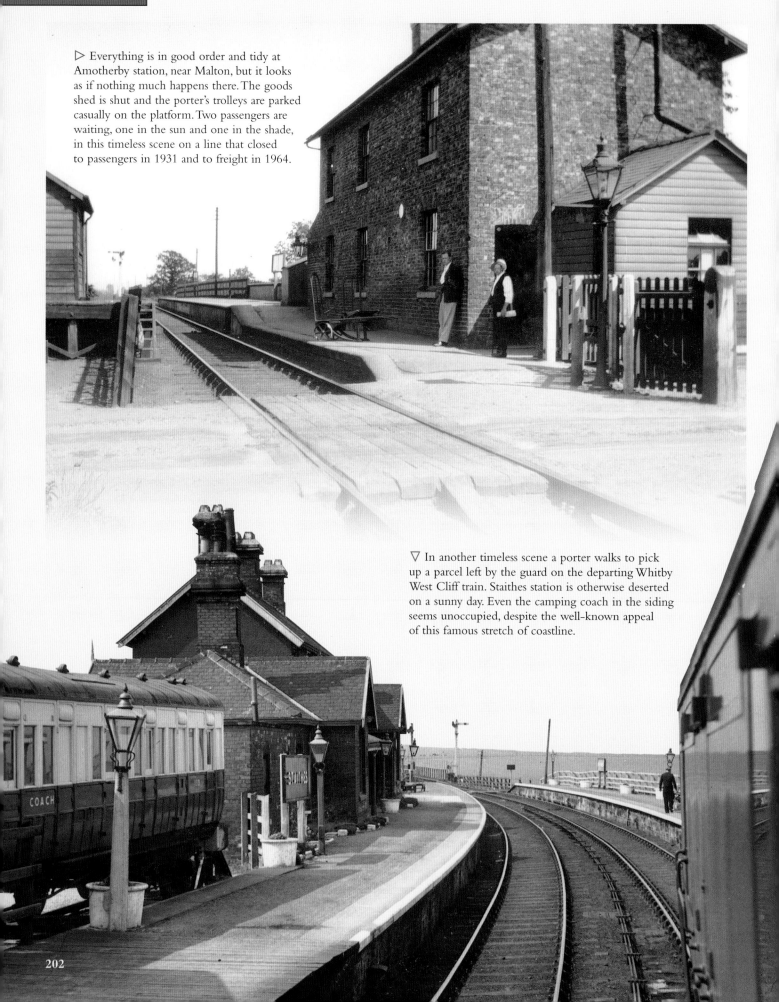

▷ Everything is in good order and tidy at Amotherby station, near Malton, but it looks as if nothing much happens there. The goods shed is shut and the porter's trolleys are parked casually on the platform. Two passengers are waiting, one in the sun and one in the shade, in this timeless scene on a line that closed to passengers in 1931 and to freight in 1964.

▽ In another timeless scene a porter walks to pick up a parcel left by the guard on the departing Whitby West Cliff train. Staithes station is otherwise deserted on a sunny day. Even the camping coach in the siding seems unoccupied, despite the well-known appeal of this famous stretch of coastline.

▷ Swinging his tea can in his hand and looking back towards the station building, the driver, his duties over, walks away from his old tank locomotive and its ancient single carriage, still marked ER. It is the late 1940s on the remote Easingwold branch in North Yorkshire and there seem, as so often, to be no passengers for the next journey along the 2½-mile line to Alne.

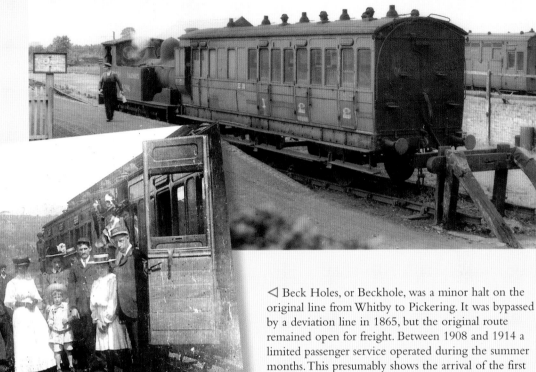

◁ Beck Holes, or Beckhole, was a minor halt on the original line from Whitby to Pickering. It was bypassed by a deviation line in 1865, but the original route remained open for freight. Between 1908 and 1914 a limited passenger service operated during the summer months. This presumably shows the arrival of the first of these holiday specials in 1908. The line is now part of the preserved North York Moors Railway.

▽ Airmyn & Rawcliffe was a surprisingly substantial and rather elegant timber station to the south of Selby. By the 1950s, when this photograph was taken, it was little used, though still in good order and smartly painted. A solitary member of staff stands on the broad wooden platform checking the waiting train, while another young man peers from the ticket office, watching the photographer.

ALONG HOLIDAY LINES

Railways came early to the North of England and a number of resorts, including Bridlington, Scarborough and Morecambe, benefited from railway connections before 1850. Others soon followed as the major companies – the London & North Western, the Lancashire & Yorkshire and the Great Northern – expanded their networks to meet the demand for holiday traffic. Coastal routes came first, but it was not long before the Lakes and the Pennines were penetrated. This pattern of expansion continued through the 19th century, and many resorts remained dependent on railway connections until the 1960s. The railways did everything to promote and exploit their services.

◁ A number of railway companies were early publishers of maps and guides. These were designed to promote both the routes and the destinations, often including information about hotels. By the 1920s annual comprehensive regional guides were widely used, their publication subsequently being maintained by British Railways.

▷ Holiday guides were supported by many special fares and Holiday Runabout tickets for short-term use over a choice of routes. The 1963 leaflet details 15 areas in the Northeast. The 1956 ticket covers Area 23, York and the coast.

BRITISH RAILWAYS

HOLIDAY GUIDE
EASTERN and NORTH EASTERN REGIONS

1/-   1949

0651   11 SEP 1956

BRITISH TRANSPORT COMMISSION (N)
Holiday Runabout Ticket
NOT TRANSFERABLE

AREA No. 23   THIRD CLASS
Rate 22/06

Available between the Stations shown on the other side by the routes indicated

UNTIL
17 SEP 1956

NOT TRANSFERABLE. Issued subject to the Regulations and Conditions in the Commission's Publications and Notices applicable to British Railways.
This ticket is not valid unless signed by the holder on the line provided.
Issued at WHITBY TOWN

Issuing Clerk.

This Ticket must be given up on expiry

14

HULL DISTRICT   FOLDER No 1

HOLIDAY
RUNABOUT TICKETS
IN NORTH EASTERN ENGLAND

7 days unlimited travel   in selected holiday districts

BRITISH RAILWAYS
NORTH EASTERN REGION

EXPLORE COAST AND COUNTRY
WHEN YOU LIKE - WHERE YOU LIKE
AS OFTEN AS YOU LIKE

ISSUED ANY DAY OF THE WEEK 28th APRIL TO 26th OCTOBER 1963

19 APR 196

▷ ▽ The first railway reached Blackpool in 1846, and by 1900 trains were bringing 3 million visitors a year to the town. The tower and the illuminations were a big draw.

CENTRAL PROMENADE, BLACKPOOL ILLUMINATIONS.

5872

The greatest free show on earth!

BLACKPOOL
ILLUMINATIONS
Inclusive

CHEAP WEEK-END
EXCURSIONS BY RAIL

Leaving on FRIDAY evenings 6th, 13th and 20th SEPTEMBER—returning from BLACKPOOL on MONDAY afternoons, 9th, 16th and 23rd SEPTEMBER, 1957

PLEASE BOOK EARLY

During the Autumn, BLACKPOOL is transformed into a glowing fairyland of scintillating light and flashing colour. Hundreds of thousands of multi-coloured lamps, hundreds of tableaux and designs, make BLACKPOOL ILLUMINATIONS a never to be forgotten spectacle.

BRITISH RAILWAYS

SPECIAL ARRANGEMENTS CAN BE MADE FOR PARTIES

British Rail
Eastern Region

1965

Southport
DELIGHT BY DAY AND NIGHT

Butlin's
HOLIDAY
CAMP
SKEGNESS
By Rail

THROUGH TRAINS ON SATURDAYS
between more than eighty towns in the Midlands, Manchester area, West Riding and SKEGNESS

IF YOU TRAVEL FROM LONDON . . .
BUTLIN'S EXPRESSES run every Saturday from King's Cross

Seats guaranteed for passengers to and from Butlin's Holiday Camp

Fill in form overleaf NOW and make sure of your FREE guaranteed seat on the HOLIDAY CAMP SPECIAL

FOR FURTHER INFORMATION ask your Station Master, Travel Agent, Divisional Manager, Great Northern House, 79/81 Euston Road, N.W.1, or Divisional Manager, Gresley House, Doncaster.

△ The holiday camp habit started in the 1930s, and many of the major holiday camps were developed with their own stations. Here, in June 1973, campers have just arrived at Filey Holiday Camp station.

◁ ▷ Butlin's were the first to appreciate the importance of direct rail connections. Many resorts also benefited from excursion specials. This upmarket LNER example is from 1939.

No. E 2344

A Buffet Car Tourist Train will run on this Half-Day Excursion (For Tariff see reverse)

TO
CLEETHORPES
RETURN FARE 4/9 THIRD CLASS

WHIT-MONDAY 29th MAY

OUTWARD JOURNEY		RETURN JOURNEY	
	a.m.		p.m.
Leeds (Central) ... dep. 11 50		Cleethorpes ... dep. 7 40	
	p.m.		p.m.
Cleethorpes ... arr. 2 30		Leeds (Central) ... arr. 10 22	

FOR CONDITIONS OF ISSUE, ETC. SEE OVER

London, April 1939.

Printed in Great Britain

L·N·E·R

BY RAIL

△ Some resorts featured rail travel in their own publicity. Typical is this leaflet issued by Southport's Town Hall Information Bureau in the early 1960s.

◁ ▽ The railways attacked the Lake District with branch lines from the south and the east, while the line from Penrith to Keswick and Cockermouth cut right across the region. Many people were outraged by what they regarded as the desecration of a glorious landscape, notably Ruskin and Wordsworth. Numerous postcards reveal how popular the area had become by the 1900s. Many, ironically, featured Wordsworth's cottage.

Dove Cottage, Grasmere.

Ambleside from Loughrigg.

DISCOVER WINDERMERE
1971
fares·services
Sealink

DISCOVER THE BEAUTY OF THE
Lake District and Cumbrian Coast
on Britain's Scenic Railway

◁ ▷ Having successfully invaded the Lake District, the railways were quick to make the most of the region's holiday potential. The Furness Railway was a notable pioneer in the promotion of the Lake District in the late Victorian era, operating steamers and issuing posters and powerful publicity. Other companies have maintained this tradition over many decades, most recently British Rail, as seen in this 1971 Windermere leaflet. In the late 1980s British Rail worked hard to promote regional travel and holiday areas with a series of local brochures, such as this 1987 Lake District and Cumbrian Coast example.

◁ ▽ Scarborough was a resort long before the railway age, but it benefited hugely from its connection to the rail network, as seen in this card, posted in 1903 by holidaymakers from South Wales. The appeal of walking in the Pennines was also significant, notably from the 1930s and into the 1960s.

SCARBOROUGH.—THE SPA PROMENADE.

▽ This evocative, although strangely deserted, 1950 view of Manchester's Victoria station shows the continuing importance of holiday traffic: the stylishly illustrated British Railways posters promote Devon and Cornwall, Scotland, Wales, the Isle of Man, Guernsey and the Lancashire coast.

CONDUCTED RAMBLES From MANCHESTER WINTER 1959/60

YOUR 1950 HOLIDAY

BRITISH RAILWAYS

APPLY AT STATIONS AND AGENCIES FOR DETAILS OF TRAIN SERVICES AND FARES

TO PLATFORMS 12.13.14.15.16 & 17

ALONG PRESERVED LINES

Opened in 1973 from Grosmont to Pickering along a line whose history dates back to 1836, the North Yorkshire Moors Railway is famous for both its landscape and its variety of services. These now run regularly into Whitby, along 6 miles of the national rail network. On the original route there was an 1860s wrought-iron bridge, whose poor condition threatened the railway's future. The decision to replace this bridge, at a cost of £750,000, was a bold one for, while major engineering on this scale is a regular part of mainline railway maintenance, it has rarely been attempted by a preserved line. These photographs indicate that there is much more to the safe and successful operation of a heritage railway than running steam trains.

△ ◁ On Sunday 1 November 2009 the famous LNER A4 Pacific No. 60007, 'Sir Nigel Gresley', hauled the final train, the Moorlander Pullman, over the old Bridge 30. In January 2010, despite heavy snow, the old girders were removed by the 120-tonne capacity, rail-mounted crane supplied, with crew, by Volker Rail. The demolition of the bridge followed, with the railway's staff and volunteers assisting bridge experts Construction Marine Ltd.

◁ The stone abutments, which had supported the original bridge near the hamlet of Darnholm for 145 years, were retained and carefully adapted to carry the new bridge. The height of the bridge and the sharp angle of the crossing over the Eller Beck are apparent here. There are a number of crossings of the river, but most of the other bridges were stone-built.

NYMR
NORTH YORKSHIRE
MOORS RAILWAY

Bridge & Wheels Appeal

Help raise £1 million for the Moors Railway

Visit us at www.nymr.co.uk

BRIDGE & WHEELS
APPEAL

△ In February 2010, four weeks after the removal of the original girders, the new bridge beams, built by Mabey Bridge Ltd, in Chepstow, are lowered into position.

◁ At 09.15 on Saturday 27 March 2010 the first train crossed the rebuilt Bridge 30, a special from Grosmont double-headed by Standard Class No. 76079 and Class 25 diesel No. D7628. Despite the worst winter for 30 years, the bridge was handed back to the railway by the contractors, 1 hour 20 minutes ahead of schedule, ready for the main 2010 season.

Grand re-opening
Bridge 30
NYMR
27ᵗʰ March 2010

ANIMALS

The railways revolutionized the carriage of livestock, particularly from farm to market, and eventually there were over 2,400 stations with livestock-handling facilities. This trade included cattle, sheep and pigs, with numbers running into the millions each year by the Edwardian era. Dedicated livestock wagons were in service by 1848, and the trade continued in a limited way into the 1970s. The carriage of horses started earlier, and at first passengers were able to travel with their horses and carriages. Later, this traffic was largely associated with the movement of racehorses in dedicated horse boxes. Working horses were a familiar feature of railway life and in 1947 over 9,000 were in use.

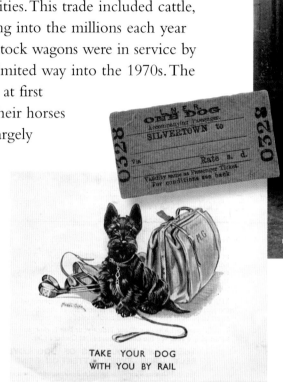

TAKE YOUR DOG
WITH YOU BY RAIL

↦ Nantymoel, the terminus of a branch line in the Welsh Valleys, was normally a quiet place but on this occasion sheep have caused some unusual excitement. Passengers watch from the train, but the men on the platform seem not to have noticed. The sheep, perhaps from a livestock wagon, seem determined to get away.

↟ ↞ Dogs could travel with their owners or unaccompanied. In the latter case, they went in the guard's van 'with chain and collar or in a receptacle'. In 1938 the rate for 150 miles was 5s (25p). Trained dogs, like Jess above, worked on large stations to collect money for railway convalescent homes.

Farrington Gurney Halt, on the Somerset line from Radstock to Bristol via Pensford, was famous for its ticket office, attached to the pub. When this was open, passengers could buy a ticket and a drink – but they had to look out for the chickens in the yard.

At Whitehaven, in Cumbria, the quays were always busy with goods traffic and the Harbour Commissioners had their own fleet of tank locomotives. This is 'King Edward VII', in about 1912. However, everything had to stop for the harbour's pet goose.

BRITISH RAILWAYS   BR. 21707

LIVE STOCK

A busy scene at Brent, in Devon, in about 1910 as horses, including Exmoor ponies, wait to be taken away to market. Ordinary horses usually travelled in cattle wagons, like those being shunted here.

Out of the ordinary

▶ *Two children pose with a magnificent heavy horse and his handler at Bentley Heath in 1913. This horse, one of over 25,000 employed by the major railway companies, worked for the Great Western and was probably used for shunting.*

◀ *The spread of horse racing during the Victorian period was entirely due to the railways, and many courses were built with dedicated rail connections for both horses and spectators. This shows a special train of horse boxes being unloaded in the 1930s at Newmarket.*

➤ *At an exhibition demonstration in the 1930s, shunting horses are cared for and shod, while in the background the crew attend to their iron horse, a smart-looking LMS Class 8F 2-8-0 locomotive.*

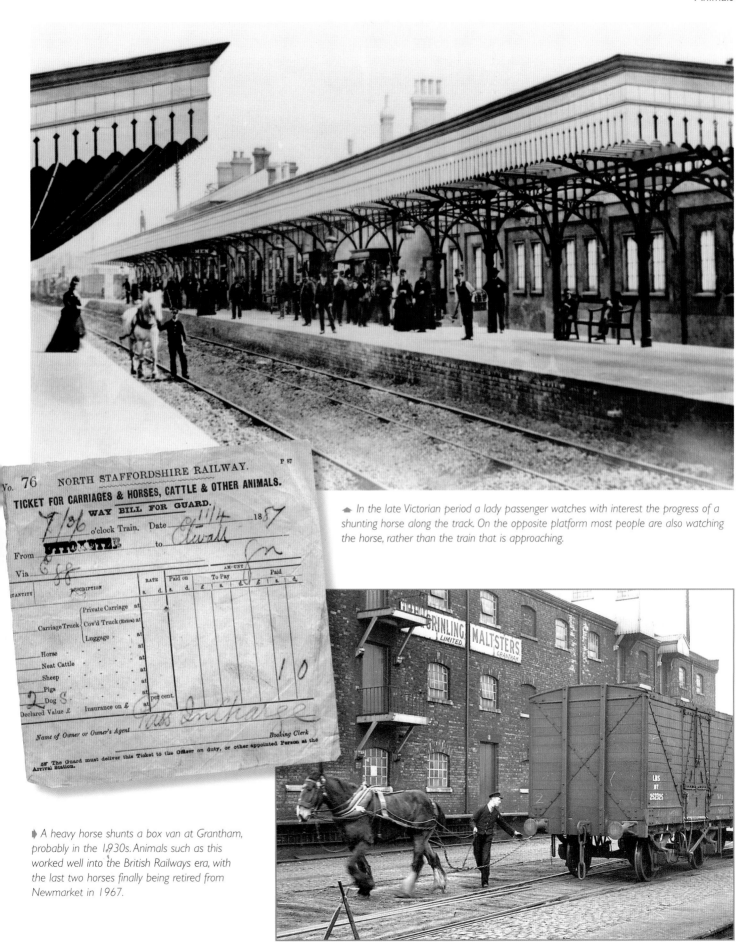

NORTH STAFFORDSHIRE RAILWAY.

TICKET FOR CARRIAGES & HORSES, CATTLE & OTHER ANIMALS.

In the late Victorian period a lady passenger watches with interest the progress of a shunting horse along the track. On the opposite platform most people are also watching the horse, rather than the train that is approaching.

A heavy horse shunts a box van at Grantham, probably in the 1930s. Animals such as this worked well into the British Railways era, with the last two horses finally being retired from Newmarket in 1967.

ANNIVERSARIES

Conscious of their history, railways have traditionally made the most of significant anniversaries. National celebrations in 1925 marking the centenary of the birth of the railways drew huge crowds and launched a sequence of similar events to commemorate the important birthdays of individual railway companies, major bridges and other structures, and even locomotives. The tradition lives on, and there is a large legacy of commemorative books and brochures, medals, tickets, photographs and other ephemera.

◄ ➡ Many railway centenaries, both major and minor, were celebrated during the 1930s and 1940s, resulting in some memorable exhibitions and brochures. The ticket was issued for the centenary of the Royal Albert Bridge in 1959.

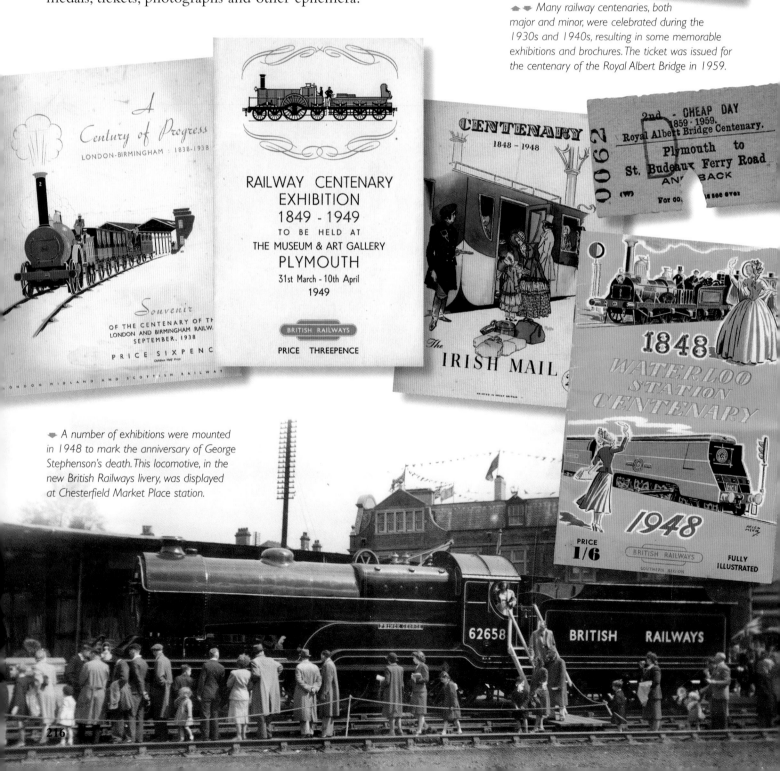

➡ A number of exhibitions were mounted in 1948 to mark the anniversary of George Stephenson's death. This locomotive, in the new British Railways livery, was displayed at Chesterfield Market Place station.

▶ Although it was quite a small, local line, and built in several sections, the Weardale Railway produced a handsome brochure to mark its centenary in 1947. This promoted the local region, as well as railway history.

☛ Some narrow gauge lines held their own celebrations; this brochure, for example, was issued in 1963, the centenary of steam on the Festiniog. Far greater were the nationwide celebrations – the last on this scale to be organized by British Rail – to mark 150 years of the GWR.

Presented as a supplement to Railway World, August 1963

FESTINIOG RAILWAY COMPANY

Centenary of Steam

1863—1963

VISIT OF
REPRESENTATIVES OF THE P
WEDNESDAY, 22nd MAY, 19

GREAT WESTERN RAILWAY'S

1985
ANNIVERSARY CELEBRATIONS
EVENTS
AND ATTRACTIONS

BRITISH RAIL (WESTERN REGION)
English Tourist Board

WEARDALE RAILWAY CENTENARY
1847 ♦♦♦ 1947
PRICE 2'6

▲ A vintage LB&SC Terrier tank locomotive and an old SE&CR carriage came together on 6 August 1956 to commemorate the centenary of the Caterham Railway, a short line in Surrey fiercely fought over by those two Victorian rivals.

FIRST DAY OF ISSUE

13 AUG 1975
SOUTHAMPTON

COMMEMORATING THE
150TH ANNIVERSARY
STOCKTON & DARLINGTON
RAILWAY

SOUTH WEST TRAINS
SOUVENIR PLATFORM TICKET
150th ANNIVERSARY OF THE
PORTSMOUTH DIRECT LINE
13th April 2009   (5657)   (M.F.)
Price 20p.   Not valid on trains.
0403

▲ Some preserved lines have now been running long enough to have significant anniversaries to celebrate. Here, in 1985, a cake is ceremonially cut to mark 25 years of the Bluebell Railway in Sussex.

▶ 1975 saw a major exhibition to mark 150 years of railways, echoing the 1925 celebrations, and special stamps were issued, seen here on one of a number of first-day covers.

HIGH DAYS & HOLIDAYS

Special occasions feature prominently in railway history, notably in the celebrations that usually accompanied the openings of lines, or sections of lines, and stations. This process started in 1825 with the opening of the Stockton & Darlington Railway and is still continuing. Other popular railway events include the introduction of new services or locomotives, with the latter sometimes combined with naming ceremonies, the visits of important people such as politicians, sporting events and outings by special interest groups that involved the railway. From the very early days, railway companies have also been conscious of the value of good publicity, so exhibitions, displays, special journeys and other promotional activities have frequently been organized with the aim of making railways, and all they represent, popular with the press, and thus with the public.

➤ In 1928 the LNER operated the first non-stop service between London Kings Cross and Edinburgh. The locomotive was 'The Flying Scotsman'. Here, before the start, the Lord Mayor of London, Sir Nigel Gresley (in bowler hat) and Driver Pibworth pose on the footplate, watched by excited spectators.

▶ In June 1933, at London's Euston station, the LMS launched to the press a new class of giant express locomotive. Designed by William Stanier, they were later known as the Princess Class. This is the first, 6200, at this stage unnamed. Thirteen were built to haul London-to-Glasgow expresses; two survive in preservation.

Locomotive naming ceremonies were often an excuse for major celebrations. This shows the unveiling with military splendour of the nameplate, 'Royal Scots Grey', on Deltic diesel No. D9000 at Edinburgh in June 1962. This locomotive worked the centenary run of The Flying Scotsman and has since been preserved.

Funeral procession of late Dr Barnardo leaving Barkingside Rv Stn

◆ Birth, life and death were all part of the railway universe, and railway funerals were often grand occasions. This shows the funeral procession for Dr Barnardo, complete with brass band, leaving Barkingside station in 1905. He lived and died at Surbiton, but his Children's Church had been opened at Barkingside in 1894.

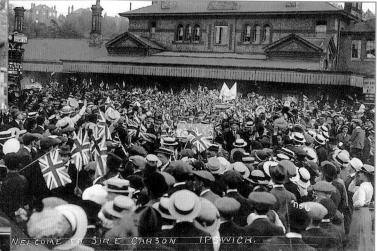

WELCOME TO SIR E. CARSON IPSWICH.

◆ The Irish Question was a major and very divisive issue of the early 1900s. Here crowds welcoming Sir Edward Carson on a visit to Ipswich by train demonstrate the huge public support for his campaign against Home Rule.

◆ In the Edwardian era it was usual for Prime Ministers to travel by train. Here, Herbert Asquith, walking with a stick behind Lady Asquith, arrives at Earlston, north of St Boswells, in the Scottish Borders. Premier from 1908 to 1916, he was MP for East Fife from 1886.

➤ An important event in naval history was the launch of HMS Dreadnought at Portsmouth in February 1906. With its route lined by sailors presenting arms, the royal train, hauled by a dockyard locomotive, makes its way slowly towards the great new battleship.

Scenes at the launch of HMS Dreadnought by the King at Portsmouth, February 1906

The Catrine branch line, near Mauchline in Ayrshire, was one of the last to be built in Britain. Built by the Glasgow & South Western Railway, it opened on 1 September 1903. Here, a carefully assembled group of elegant ladies, officials and small girls celebrate the opening. The short line closed to passengers in 1943.

A much larger crowd, spilling onto the tracks at Epworth station, await the arrival of the first train on the Axholme Joint Railway in 1904. Although it offered a link between the North Eastern and the Lancashire & Yorkshire networks, it was never very busy, and closed to passengers in 1933.

Harrogate Corporation's new Roundhill reservoir, built at a cost of £500,000, was opened in 1913. Perhaps this is a view of the opening ceremony, with the engineers, Corporation officials and their guests posing with a train on the 7-mile, 2ft gauge light railway that ran from Masham to the reservoir.

Crowds have gathered on the platform at Seven Sisters station in Glamorgan to await the special train taking them to Neath Fair. It is in the Edwardian era and everyone has dressed for the occasion. Now established for over 700 years, the fair is held in September.

Women and children from St Andrew's Church, Fulham, mostly dressed in white, fill the platform at Kensington station while they wait for the train to take them on their day outing to the Bricketts Wood amusement park in Hertfordshire.

BRITISH RAILWAYS

B. 25866

INTERNATIONAL FOOTBALL MATCH
ENGLAND
VERSUS
SCOTLAND
AT WEMBLEY STADIUM
SATURDAY, 11th APRIL, 1959

SPECIAL CAFETERIA CAR
DAY EXCURSIONS TO
LONDON
ON
FRIDAY NIGHT, 10th APRIL

From GLASGOW

OUTWARD	Train No W. 541	Train No C. 604	RETURN (early morning, Sunday 12th April)	Train No W. 541	Train No C. 604
	p.m.	p.m.		a.m.	a.m.
Glasgow (Central) ... leave	8 55	....	London (Euston) ... leave	1 10	....
Glasgow (St. Enoch) .. ,,	....	....	London (St. Pancras) ,,	....	0
London (Euston) ... arrive	6 23a	....	Glasgow (St. Enoch) arrive	10 32	12 31p
London (St. Pancras) ,,	....	7 10s			

SECOND **80/-** RETURN

From PAISLEY

OUTWARD	Train No C. 604	RETURN (early morning, Sunday 12th April)	Train No C. 604
	p.m.		a.m.
Paisley (Gilmour Street) ... leave	8 22	London (St. Pancras) ... leave	....
London (St. Pancras) ... arrive	7 10s	Paisley (Gilmour Street) ... arrive	12 13p

SECOND **80/-** RETURN

The tickets are only valid on the dates and by the trains specified

(over

For decades, football specials were a feature of railway life, with thousands of supporters being transported to and from football grounds every Saturday through the season. Internationals also attracted huge crowds. For the England vs Scotland game at Wembley in April 1959, special overnight trains with cafeteria cars ran between Glasgow or Paisley and London, allowing supporters a full day in London.

Many racecourses throughout Britain either had dedicated stations or were well served by the railways, and excursion trains ran to many race meetings. This handbill lists some of those operating in May and June 1961. One of the best-known racecourse stations was opened at Newbury by the Great Western in 1905, with platforms directly connected to the track. This shows a meeting in the Edwardian era, when the station was newly built. Today, it is one of the few racecourse stations still in use.

PLEASE RETAIN FOR REFERENCE

RACE MEETINGS
1st MAY to 10th JUNE 1961

PROGRAMME
OF
DAY EXCURSIONS
FIRST AND SECOND CLASS

NOTTINGHAM	1st MAY and 3rd JUNE
CHESTER	2nd, 3rd and 4th MAY
LEICESTER	8th and 9th MAY
RIPON	10th MAY
UTTOXETER	11th and 22nd MAY
HAYDOCK PARK	12th and 13th MAY
WOLVERHAMPTON	13th MAY
YORK	16th, 17th and 18th MAY
DONCASTER	20th and 22nd MAY
BIRMINGHAM	22nd and 23rd MAY
THIRSK	26th and 27th MAY
CARLISLE	1st JUNE
PONTEFRACT	10th JUNE

Travel in Rail Comfort

LONDON MIDLAND

E277/ADEX

British Railways inherited the Camping Coach idea from the Big Four and were keen to develop the network as part of their holiday business. A typical coach was displayed at Paddington station in January 1953 to encourage public interest. Here, after a hard day's work, the promotional staff involved settle down to a meal cooked in the kitchen, at the end of the carriage.

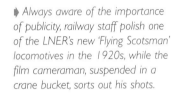

Always aware of the importance of publicity, railway staff polish one of the LNER's new 'Flying Scotsman' locomotives in the 1920s, while the film cameraman, suspended in a crane bucket, sorts out his shots.

A richly decorated Highland Railway locomotive, No.11, 'Blair Castle', complete with mounted stag's head, is ready for the day's duties, hauling a Grand Press Tour to some of the most northerly parts of the network. Promotion and carefully controlled publicity were always important, even in the Victorian era.

GOING OVERSEAS

Railways began to operate steamer services from the early 1850s, and, thanks to the many competing companies, the routes quickly proliferated. Services operated across the Channel to France, to northern Europe via the North Sea, and to Ireland. In all, between the 1850s and 1984 – when all the British Rail shipping interests were disposed of – more than 50 companies owned about 1,200 ships of all kinds, including passenger and cargo vessels, river steamers, tugs and dredgers. Some companies owned the ports from which they sailed and ran dedicated boat trains to service their ships. Promotion and publicity featured large, notably in the British Railways era.

▶ ➡ *The Golden Arrow, the most famous of all Pullman services, linked London and Paris with a journey time, including the Channel ferry, of under seven hours. Famous in the 1930s, it was quickly brought back after World War II. This photograph shows the Golden Arrow leaving from Victoria in about 1947, hauled by a smart Merchant Navy Class locomotive, 'Channel Packet'. Many other services linked London with Paris and these were extensively promoted.*

THE FRENCH PORTS AND

PARIS

SERVICES AND FARES

SUMMER 1955   BRITISH RAILWAYS   22 MAY - 1 OCT. incl.

THE PULLMAN
CAR COMPANY LIMITED

For conditions see inside cover.
Voir les conditions de transport au verso.
Für Bedingungen siehe Rückseite des Umschlages

BRITISH RAILWAYS
CHEMINS DE FER BRITANNIQUES
BRITISCHE

SLEEP
YOUR
WAY TO
BRUSSELS

THE
REGULAR
SERVICE
YOU
CAN
RELY
ON

British Railways

27 MAY 1962
TO 25 M...
INCLUSI...

NIGHT FERRY

BRITISH AND FRENCH RAILWAYS
present the

NIGHT FERRY

WITH

THROUGH SLEEPING CARS

NIGHTLY

			arr.	↑ 7.45*
22.00	dep.	LONDON (VICTORIA)		
8.44 ↓	arr.	PARIS (GARE DU NORD)	dep.	22.00

*7.35 on Saturdays and Sundays

NOW IN ITS 41st YEAR

"An excellent performance—one is quite transported."
"The sleeping car attendant played his part extremely well . . ."
". . . an international cast . . . an overnight success."

TICKET PRICES
LONDON-PARIS

One way fare including "Single" sleeper   £55.80
One way fare including berth in
"Double" sleeper   £35.00

Book in advance through principal British Rail stations and Travel
Centres or rail appointed travel agents.

◆ ☛ The only passenger train
that actually crossed the Channel
was the night ferry, with through
sleeping cars linking London with
Paris and Brussels. This first ran
in 1936, using train ferries on
the Dover-to-Dunkirk route. It
was extensively, and imaginatively,
advertised in its later years
because of increasing competition
from air traffic, and it continued
to operate into the 1970s.

THE Riviera
BY TRAIN AND SHIP

SERVICES AND FARES
26 MAY TO 28 SEPTEMBER 1963 INCLUSIVE

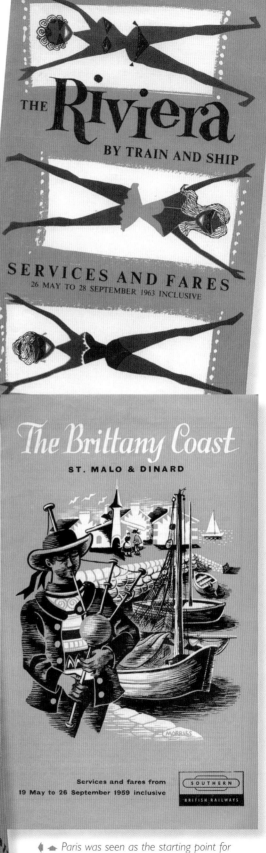

The Brittany Coast
ST. MALO & DINARD

Services and fares from
19 May to 26 September 1959 inclusive

SOUTHERN
BRITISH RAILWAYS

No. 10 OF A SERIES

Spain & Portugal
by train and ship

SERVICES AND FARES
26 May to 28 September 1963 inclusive

◆ ☛ Paris was seen as the starting point for
a great variety of journeys around Europe by
train, and through the 1950s and 1960s British
Railways produced a wide range of colourful
brochures to encourage European travel for
pleasure. While many featured destinations
in France, Spain and Portugal, others included
Greece, Yugoslavia and Scandinavia.

ENGLAND
AND THE
CONTINENT
BY SHORT
SEA
ROUTES
1933.

SOUTHERN
RAILWAY

Sea Ferry Services
TO AND FROM THE CONTINENT AND CHANNEL ISLANDS
FOR CARS AND MOTOR CYCLES

Lander

ATES & FARES FOR ALL ROUTES   BRITISH RAILWAYS

1st JANUARY to 31st DECEMBER 1959 inclusive

Competition between railway companies and cross-Channel routes resulted in a vast range of colourful guide books, brochures, leaflets and timetables, often reflecting the graphic styles of their period. Initially these promoted passenger travel for holidays and excursions, but from the 1930s the emphasis switched to the car ferry. The Channel Islands were always popular – and in 1967 British Rail had a special offer for honeymooners.

The
Normandy
Coast
VIA NEWHAVEN-DIEPPE

JUNE, 1895.

LONDON BRIGHTON & SOUTH COAST
&
WESTERN of FRANCE RAILWAYS

THE
NEWHAVEN
DIEPPE

AND ROUEN ROUTE TO
The Continent.

CARS & MOTOR-CYCLES
TO AND FROM
THE CONTINENT
AND
CHANNEL ISLANDS

LESLIE CARR

SERVICES, RATES AND FARES
BY ALL ROUTES

OCTOBER 21st, 1951,
until further notice.

BRITISH RAILWAYS

May 27 to
September 29, 1962

SANDS ACROSS THE SEA

BRITTANY NORMANDY PICARDY

1/s-

SOUTHERN RAILWAY

Excursions
from Folkestone and Dover to
**Boulogne, le Touquet,
Calais, Dunkerque,
Ostend, Bruges,
Ghent and Brussels**

Summer 1970
PASSPORTS NOT REQUIRED
(British subjects and citizens of the Irish Republic only)

Sealink

SPECIAL OFFER!
**Honeymoon
in Guernsey**
25 MARCH – 8 APRIL 1967

British Rail
Southern Region

in association with
Guernsey Hotels and
Guest Houses Association

➤ Railway companies operated special boat train services to ports such as Dover, Folkestone, Newhaven, Harwich and Holyhead, and many continued to run through the British Railways era. Here, in June 1964, a startled Ford van driver comes face to face with a diesel locomotive hauling a boat train along the Weymouth tramway from the quay.

Lancashire & Yorkshire and North Eastern Railways.

DIRECT EXPRESS ROUTE TO THE CONTINENT VIA HULL AND ZEEBRUGGE

Time Table JUNE 28th to OCTOBER 3rd, 1913.

Spend a Day in Eire!!

LONG DAY TRIPS
FROM
EUSTON
TO
DUBLIN
Via HOLYHEAD & DUN LAOGHAIRE
EACH FRIDAY NIGHT
12th OCTOBER until 30th NOVEMBER 1956

SECOND CLASS THROUGHOUT
70/6
SALOON ON STEAMER 20/- EXTRA

CHILDREN under three years of age, free : three years and under fourteen, half-fare.

Hull was the major North Sea port, with services to Hamburg and other German destinations, Rotterdam, Belgium and Copenhagen. Other routes operated from Grimsby and Goole. Better known were services across the Irish sea. Special promotions included day trips to Dublin from London, and in 1960 midweek services operated on seven routes.

For a week or a fortnight
TRAVEL MID-WEEK
CHEAP
MID-WEEK HOLIDAY RETURN TICKETS
will be available as indicated herein between
3RD MAY & 27TH OCTOBER 1960
from all Western Region Stations to Ports and selected stations in
IRELAND
VIA
FISHGUARD-ROSSLARE
FISHGUARD-CORK (Direct)
HOLYHEAD-DUN LAOGHAIRE
HEYSHAM-BELFAST
LIVERPOOL-BELFAST
LIVERPOOL-DUBLIN
STRANRAER-LARNE

in conjunction with . . . .
BELFAST STEAMSHIP CO. LTD.
BRITISH & IRISH STEAM PACKET CO. LTD.
CITY OF CORK STEAM PACKET CO. LTD.
CORAS IOMPAIR EIREANN
ULSTER TRANSPORT AUTHORITY

Holyhead was the earliest and the most important departure point for Ireland. This Edwardian image of frenetic activity shows an LNWR boat train for London getting ready to depart.

SEND YOUR GOODS BY THE NEW
S.R. TRAIN-FERRY

Fast through Goods Train Services
to and from all parts of Europe
(France, Switzerland, Italy, Spain, Austria, etc.).
Unloading at the Ports avoided.

SPEEDY TRANSIT · NO TRANSHIPMENT

LAURENCE DUNN

TRAIN FERRY, HARWICH. (H.8)

TRAIN FERRIES

Harwich

Dover.

Zeebrugge.

Dunkerque

FOR TRADE WITH
THE CONTINENT

ISLE OF MAN
Holiday Paradise!

For train services and fares, enquire at
Stations, Offices and Agencies

·BRITISH RAILWAYS·

The train ferry, designed primarily for freight, was developed during World War I and scheduled services continued to operate until the opening of the Channel Tunnel. The Southern Railway ferry, above, carried goods wagons; the night ferry took carriages, cars and lorries. The Edwardian card below shows Heysham, a port for Ireland and the Isle of Man.

HEYSHAM DOCKS

ACCIDENTS

Disasters, and their causes, have been a recurring theme throughout railway history, matched by ever more demanding government legislation designed both to improve safety and to establish the cause of incidents involving death, injury or damage. Major accidents have always been comprehensively reported by newspapers, encouraging a macabre fascination on the part of the public that has continued to the present day. As a result, these are all well documented; in many cases, in fact, souvenir postcards were issued. But equally fascinating to the public were the minor incidents that seemed to occur with alarming regularity. Whatever the scale of the accident, what is notable in so many of these photographs is the presence of spectators very much closer to the accident scene than modern regulations would allow.

◆ The cause of an accident could be anything from mechanical failure, track problems or signalling to natural elements such as weather, and – inevitably the most common and the hardest to anticipate or control – human error. The photograph above shows the after-effects of a serious collision between a coal train and a passenger train near Pontypridd in 1911.

◗ Minor incidents, especially derailments, are not uncommon, and luckily most cause only local disruption. On the Tyne Improvement Commission Railway system in the 1950s, four loaded coal hoppers have been derailed at the points while being shunted by an industrial tank locomotive. The breakdown train has arrived and railwaymen are discussing what to do next.

ailed N. Walsham

⬧ In typical fashion a minor derailment at North Walsham, Norfolk, in the early 1900s has quickly become a matter of great local interest. Crowds have arrived, including children in their holiday best, and the photographer has assembled them in front of his camera. The image was issued as a postcard.

⬤ Spectators have quickly gathered to enjoy the chaos created by the derailment of a goods train at Halwill Junction, Devon, in the summer of 1905. This would have caused considerable disruption on the busy LSWR holiday routes to Bude and Padstow.

Out of the ordinary

♦ A postcard records the derailment of a mineral train at Kirkby Stephen, Cumbria, in 1909. Here, the spectators include women, young men in boaters and a bicyclist.

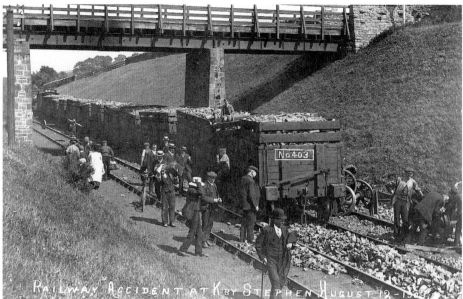

MR FRED FLEETWOOD, Driver of the Scotch Express, killed in the Terrible Railway Accident at Grantham, on Wednesday, Sept. 19th. 1906.

▲ The causes of the Grantham rail disaster of 19 September 1906, when 14 people died, have never been clearly established. The driver, Fred Fleetwood, commemorated by this postcard, was among the dead. Strangely, the card was posted in York three years after the event and the message makes no mention of the disaster.

▲ The breakdown train is hard at work at Diggle, near Oldham, in 1923, following a derailment. Spectators crowd the opposite bank and the bridge.

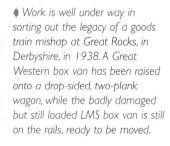

♦ Work is well under way in sorting out the legacy of a goods train mishap at Great Rocks, in Derbyshire, in 1938. A Great Western box van has been raised onto a drop-sided, two-plank wagon, while the badly damaged but still loaded LMS box van is still on the rails, ready to be moved.

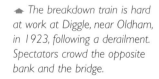

◆ A combination of an unstable locomotive and some poor trackwork caused a high-speed derailment at Sevenoaks, Kent, in August 1927. The last coach of the train is closest to the camera, and the engine and other coaches are piled up against the bridge in the distance. Thirteen people were killed.

➥ The recovery of the vehicles is often the most interesting part of any railway incident. Here, another postcard, issued some time after the event, shows the huge crowds that had gathered to watch the recovery of a locomotive that had left the track at Gretna in 1901 and fallen from the embankment.

➥ The aftermath of a disaster near Hitchin, Hertfordshire, in 1953 is all too apparent in this photograph, with goods wagons piled on top of the locomotive. Yet there is time for the young man to lean on his spade and pose for the camera before he starts to clear it all up.

GRETNA RAILWAY ACCIDENT. MAY 1901.
RAISING THE ENGINE.

FINAL JOURNEYS

L ine closures have long been a feature of railway history, with a number of examples dating from the 1840s and 1850s. Lack of use and the opening of more direct routes were the usual reasons for closing a line. In total, about 400 miles of line were closed before 1910, while over 2,700 miles disappeared between 1922 and 1953. However, the major closure programme, which directly changed or affected the lives of ordinary people the length and breadth of Britain, followed the publication of Dr Beeching's report in 1963. This resulted in the loss of thousands of miles of railway, 2,000 stations and thousands of jobs. In the early days, closures passed largely unnoticed, but by the Beeching era many were marked by legal battles, special trains and huge crowds of passengers and spectators, especially to commemorate the last day and the last train.

➥ *Scotland was particularly hard hit by closures, both in the early days and in the post-Beeching era. Here, a large crowd has gathered to see the last passenger train on the Lauder branch, a remote line to the southeast of Edinburgh. This was a special run by the Branch Line Society on 15 November 1958, well before Beeching. Such a scene, commonplace at that time, and with not a single high-visibility jacket to be seen, is inconceivable in the age of Health and Safety. Note the stationmaster standing with enthusiasts on the locomotive's buffer beam!*

MONMOUTH and its RAILWAYS
Photographic Souvenir and Historical Notes
in connection with the
LAST PASSENGER TRAIN
on the
MONMOUTH - ROSS and MONMOUTH - CHEPSTOW
branches of the Western Region of British Railways
(formerly Great Western Railway)
SUNDAY, 4th JANUARY, 1959

Organised by
THE STEPHENSON LOCOMOTIVE SOCIETY
(Midland Area)
being the first Rail-Tour of the Golden Jubilee Year of the Society

◀ Another early closure was the line from Stafford to Uttoxeter, with passenger services ceasing in 1939. It remained open for goods, and in 1957 an enthusiasts' special, seen here pausing at Ingestre and Weston station, was the last passenger train to use the line.

▶ ➤ When the Crystal Palace, built to house the Great Exhibition of 1851, was reopened at Sydenham in 1854, a branch line was built to serve it. It had a grand terminus station, which became known as Crystal Palace High Level. The photograph above right shows the extensive sidings, on the final day of service, 19 September 1954. The last train into the station was a special hauled by 31576, an ancient C Class locomotive dating back to the 1900s. Below, it is seen being turned, prior to the final journey back to the main line.

➡ The Isle of Wight's distinctive network remained a steam railway to its end in 1966, and its demise was much lamented by enthusiasts, with many special events and services. The network was operated by Class 02 tank engines, a design dating back to 1889. This is No. 27, 'Merstone', the last to be steamed by British Rail, and seen here decorated accordingly.

WIGHT LOCOMOTIVE SOCIETY

PAYS ITS LAST

RESPECTS

LAST '02'
Steamed by BR

27

LAST TRAIN
WELSHPOOL &
LLANFAIR LINE
3ʳᵈ NOV 1956

◆ Closures affected both major and minor railways, and narrow gauge lines did not escape the axe. November 1956 saw the last train on the Welshpool & Llanfair Railway, seen here on departure with passengers crammed into goods wagons. The railway has since been reopened as a tourist line.

The inscription painted on the side of Class 2MT tank locomotive No. 41225 says it all. Cross-country routes, by then little used, were easy victims for the closure planners.

BEDFORD - NORTHAMPTON
BORN. JUNE. 10ᵀᴴ 1872
DIED. MARCH. 3ᴿᴰ 1962
R.I.P

Wath-on-Dearne, or Wath Central, was on a Great Central line north of Sheffield. It was closed in 1959 but only one enthusiast, camera at the ready, seems to have turned out to see the last train. Wath had two other stations, one for the Midland Railway and one for the Hull & Barnsley.

A gleaming member of GWR's 4500 Class takes on water at Bromyard station on 26 April 1958, prior to hauling the last train from Bromyard to Leominster, a Stephenson Locomotive Society special. Crowds on the platform await the departure.

COME TO SCOTLAND.

CLEAR
BRACING
AIR

ARDROS

SAL

TURNBERRY
GOLF
COURSES
TURNBE
STAT

GIRVAN

To STRANRAER

MI

FOR YOUR HOLIDAYS
BY THE WEST COAST ROUTE.

LONDON & NORTH WESTERN & CALEDONIAN RAILWAYS.

To see the
d o'Burns

DALRY

_TO PAISLEY AND
GLASGOW (ST.ENOCH)_

TO GLASGOW (ST.ENOCH)

ATS

KILMARNOCK

RIVER IRVINE

IRVINE

TROON

MAUCHLINE

PRESTWICK

AYR

RIVER AYR

TARBOLTON

LUGAR W.

MUI

_BURNS
COTTAGE_

ALLOWAY
STATION

_BR.O'R_ _BURNS_
DOON _MONUMENT_

OCHILTREE
STATION

W. OF COYLE

BURNOCK W.

CU

RIVER DOON

RKOSWALD

IN AND AROUND

SCOTLAND

_BOGTON
L._
NESS GLEN

DALMELL

_LOCH
DOON_

TRAVEL BY THE

LAND & G.&S.W. RYS.

E ONLY DIRECT ROUTE

STATION SCENES

The Scottish railway map was determined largely by geography. The main lines linking the primary cities were built quite quickly, followed by their local networks. Routes serving remoter regions, particularly in the north, were generally built later, and often at great expense, but the two main companies, the Caledonian and the Highland, were determined to build lines to serve as much of Scotland as possible. One of the results was a wealth of branch lines, most of which were lost in the 1950s and 1960s. Today, while most of the primary routes have survived, vast areas of Scotland are without any rail service. The real story is told, as ever, by photographs, and these show the diverse nature of both routes and stations.

△ The main line to Stranraer via Castle Douglas was completed in 1862, and this became one of the primary routes for shipping services to Ireland. Stranraer is still a busy port, but it is now served by a roundabout route via Ayr. This is Stranraer Town station, on the line to Portpatrick, which closed in 1965.

▽ The Stranraer line passed through remote countryside for much of its route. Typical of the small, rural stations was New Galloway, seen here in the early 20th century with cars waiting to take visitors on tours around nearby Loch Ken.

▽ A smart stone station was built in the 1860s in Kirkcudbright, as the terminus for the branch line to the town from Castle Douglas. The line closed completely in 1965.

PERTH STATION, THE 11.50 A.M. HIGHLAND EXPRESS
ABOUT TO START FOR INVERNESS.

1115

△ Perth, or Perth General as it used to be, is one of Scotland's most important stations. As a gateway to the north of the country it was, from the late 1800s, very busy in summer with visitors to the Highlands. In this 1920s view an Inverness express is about to depart.

▽ The Callander & Oban Railway was built by a fiercely independent and ambitious company, but it was not until 1880 that funds were found to complete the line, begun in 1865. On this day in the early 1900s, the carriages at Callander are doing good trade.

◁ Two Edwardian ladies and their Jack Russell wait for a train on Lundin Links station, one of a number on a line that wandered along the coast of Fife from Leuchars. Both have cameras at the ready.

▽ An elegant lady poses on the platform at Fortrose, the terminus of a branch along the north shore of the Moray Firth. There seem to be no other passengers travelling to the main line at Muir of Ord.

241

△ The glorious scenery around Killin station is apparent, but if the young man who is posing so casually in this 1967 photograph needs a train, he will have a long wait. The passenger service had ceased two years earlier.

▽ This 1920s view of Whistlefield Halt, north of Garelochhead, shows the splendour of its setting beside Loch Long. Today the line survives, but the station is long closed.

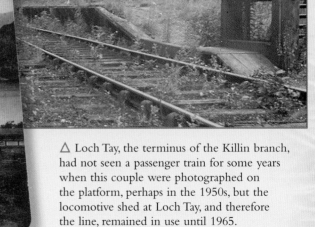

△ Loch Tay, the terminus of the Killin branch, had not seen a passenger train for some years when this couple were photographed on the platform, perhaps in the 1950s, but the locomotive shed at Loch Tay, and therefore the line, remained in use until 1965.

RAILWAY STATION, WHISTLEFIELD, LOCH LONG.

◁ In this 1910 postcard, a North British Railway West Highland Express enters Glenfinnan station, on the line from Fort William to Mallaig. This rugged line, notable for the dramatic landscape and the nearby viaduct, had been completed only nine years earlier.

▽ Under the watchful eyes of two senior railwaymen and a member of Pitlochry's station staff, two trains cross. One is on track maintenance duties, and both are headed by Class 26 diesels. It is the early 1970s, when these locomotives were widely used throughout northern Scotland.

△ In September 1960 an enthusiast and his friend, the photographer, have braved the weather and made the long journey on their motor scooters to Barcaldine Halt, on the Ballachulish branch from Connel Ferry. They have been lucky to see a veteran locomotive on duty.

▷ On a sunny May day in 1958, a special railtour organized by the Stephenson Locomotive Society has arrived at Lennoxtown, on the north Glasgow line from Kirkintilloch to Killearn. A couple of local girls, in summer frocks, have turned out to watch.

▽ In bright summer sunshine in August 1955, the branch line train from Dornoch to the mainline junction at The Mount rests at the platform while the driver has a cigarette break and his fireman loads coal into the grate. The carriage doors are open but there are no passengers. The line closed in 1960.

◁ Another branch that was little used in its later years ran to Aberfeldy from the main line at Ballinluig. Here, a couple of years before closure in 1965, the elderly tank locomotive and its single carriage wait while the station staff chat with the crew. There is not a passenger to be seen.

ALONG HOLIDAY LINES

The development of Scotland as a popular holiday destination coincided with the coming of the railways. Some of the initial inspiration came from Queen Victoria, whose frequent visits to Balmoral from the 1850s made Scotland a very fashionable place. The main lines were mostly built quite early, and then branch lines and rural routes were added to the network throughout the latter part of the 19th century, with some not being completed until the start of the 20th century. Many of these lines were driven in part by the ever-increasing numbers of people who came to Scotland for its spectacular mountains and remote beaches, the peace and quiet, and for its walking, golf and skiing. Railway resort hotels added to the appeal, and railways constantly promoted travel to Scotland and around the country.

▽ In the summer of 1965 two Standard Class locomotives double head a long holiday train over Kilpatrick viaduct near Pinmore, south of Ayr. The train is a Saturday summer special from Stranraer to Glasgow, filled with returning holidaymakers.

▷ ▽ Railway publicity has always made the most of such traditional Scottish features as the landscape, its history and tartan – the 1930s LNER brochure below was issued for the American market.

COLORFUL
ENGLAND
AND
SCOTLAND

LONDON AND NORTH
EASTERN RAILWAY

ADVANCE PROGRAMME
CIRCULAR TOURS
AND EXCURSIONS

SCOTLAND
TRAIN — MOTOR — STEAMER
SEASON 1961
BRITISH RAILWAYS

◁ ▽ The many-faceted appeal of Scotland, from mountains and beaches to classic small towns and local events such as the Highland Games, has always been at the core of railway publicity. At the same time, railway and travel companies have always worked hard to encourage holidaymakers to travel to and around Scotland by train. Typical were the many special ticket offers, while the car sleeper was also popular. In 1960 a family could take their car from London to Perth and back by train for about £30.

247

DAY OUTING for Amateur Photographers

ALL-DAY EXCURSION

BY SPECIAL TRAIN

(with Cafeteria Car)

TO THE

CENTRAL HIGHLANDS

FROM

GLASGOW, PARTICK HILL, CLYDEBANK and DUMBARTON

SATURDAY, 25th MAY, 1957

Going via Loch Long, Loch Lomond and Crianlarich to Killin—Returning via Bonnie Strathyre, Callander, Dunblane and Stirling.

Fare for the **12/6** Round Trip

(Parties of ten or more can obtain tickets at 11/- each if application is made not later than 11th May).

MAKE IT A FAMILY PARTY

Children under three years of age, free; three years and under fourteen, half-fare.

ACCOMMODATION LIMITED

BRITISH RAILWAYS

EARLY BOOKING RECOMMENDED

Relax together in SCOTLAND

A weekend at a BTH hotel and rail fares at greatly reduced prices

WINTERBREAK PACKAGE WEEKEND

BTH — British Rail

1971/1972 SEASON

B. 22062

For Stay-at-Home Fair Holidaymakers!

See T.V. ON BRITAIN'S ONLY **TELEVISION TRAIN**

ST. ANDREWS	SATURDAY 20th JULY	**14/4**
NORTH BERWICK	MONDAY 22nd JULY	**11/9**
ARBROATH	TUESDAY 23rd JULY	**16/-**
OBAN	WEDNESDAY 24th JULY	**17/6**

BRITISH RAILWAYS

leaving **GLASGOW** (Queen Street)

by the

EVENING CITIZEN SHOW TRAIN

INCLUSIVE FARE FOR THE **FOUR DAYS** **50/-**

NOTE:—A Cafeteria Car will be available on each train for the service of light refreshments.

PASSENGERS CAN SELECT ANY SINGLE OR COMBINATION OF EXCURSIONS THEY DESIRE. FOR TRAIN TIMES SEE OTHER SIDE.

FIRST CLASS ENTERTAINMENT WILL BE PROVIDED BY THE EVENING CITIZEN

TICKETS OBTAINABLE IN ADVANCE

at stations and are valid on the date for which issued and by the services specified.

Children under three years of age, free ; three years and under fourteen, half-fare.

All information regarding Excursions and Cheap Fares will be supplied on application at Stations or to E. Lees, District Passenger Manager, 50 George Square, Glasgow. Telephone—Douglas 7092.

NOTICE AS TO CONDITIONS.—These tickets are issued subject to the British Transport Commission's published Regulations and Conditions applicable to British Railways exhibited at their Stations or obtainable free of charge at station ticket offices.

B.R. 35001—EK—July, 1957

McCorquodale, Glasgow

△ ▷ As well as the usual short breaks, British Railways came up with some novel ideas to promote travel in Scotland, including photographers' outings and, bizarrely, 'Britain's only television train'.

THE NORTHERN BELLE

△ Introduced in 1933, the LNER's Northern Belle was Britain's first luxury cruise train, offering tours of northern England and Scotland. Here, on a wet day, the train has 'docked' at Balloch Pier station and the passengers, well wrapped against the weather, are setting off for their boat trip on Loch Lomond.

DISCOVER THE BEAUTY OF THE
Kyle Line
on Britain's Scenic Railway

IN THE PASS OF BRANDER

THE JOURNEY BETWEEN
EDINBURGH AND **OBAN**
BY BRITISH RAILWAYS
INTERESTING FEATURES EN ROUTE

STEAM TRAINS FROM FORT WILLIAM

MAY TO OCTOBER 1988

Steam through the Highlands and back by train
MALLAIG-SKYE

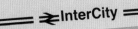

≥InterCity≥

BRITISH RAILWAYS

FREEDOM OF SCOTLAND TICKET
SEVEN DAYS UNLIMITED TRAVEL
between
ALL STATIONS ON BRITISH RAILWAYS
in
THE SCOTTISH REGION
also
STEAMER SERVICES OF THE CALEDONIAN STEAM PACKET COMPANY LTD. BETWEEN CLYDE COAST AND LOCH LOMOND PIERS

Date of Expiry

14 SEP 58

◁ △ Lineside guides, holiday and Runabout tickets, and promotional postcards were all part of the selling of Scotland by railway companies old and new. The late 1980s also saw the introduction of Britain's first scheduled mainline steam service since 1968, on the Fort William-to-Mallaig line. Still operating today, this classic steam service is now called The Jacobite.

249

ALONG PRESERVED LINES

The Strathspey Railway, one of Scotland's few preserved lines, runs from Aviemore, where there is a link with the national rail network, to Broomhill. There are plans to extend the route to Grantown-on-Spey. Among a range of events and activities organized throughout the year, the Strathspey operates special services over the Christmas period, including the Santa Express and the Mince Pie Special. Unlike most of its more southerly rivals, the Strathspey can often offer its visitors the prospect of a white Christmas. The scenes shown here are not unusual, and the great appeal to the public has to be balanced against the operational problems associated with heavy snow and freezing conditions.

▽ ▷ Headed by locomotive No. 17, an Andrew Barclay 0-6-0 built in 1935, the seasonal Mince Pie Special drifts into the platform at Boat of Garten. Deep snow adds a Christmas card flavour to the scene, but inevitably brings problems: snow has to be cleared from overhanging structures, platform edges must be made safe, and points unfrozen. It also places high demands on carriage heating.

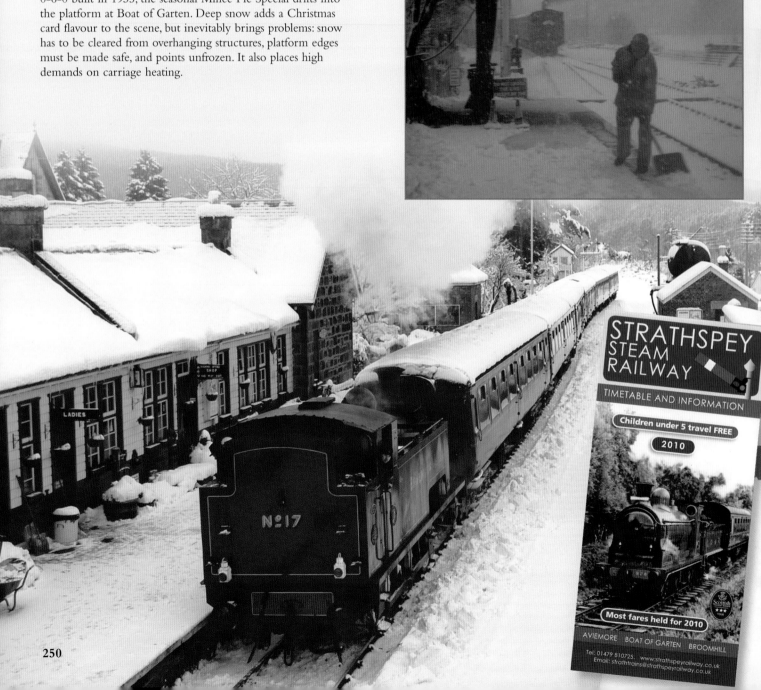

STRATHSPEY STEAM RAILWAY

TIMETABLE AND INFORMATION

Children under 5 travel FREE

2010

Most fares held for 2010

AVIEMORE · BOAT OF GARTEN · BROOMHILL

Tel: 01479 810725. www.strathspeyrailway.co.uk
Email: strathtrains@strathspeyrailway.co.uk

250

◁ The Santa Express, seen here in typical winter weather, is a popular annual event on the railway. In fact, there are so many Santa Expresses running on preserved lines all over Britain that Father Christmas must have his work cut out.

▽ For many people the Strathspey's Christmas specials are an integral part of the festive season, and the snow is part of the experience. This is Broomhill station.

▷ A visit by Father Christmas is a guaranteed part of any trip on the Santa Express. Here, in a suitably decorated carriage, he prepares to hand out presents from his sack to all children taking part in this journey through a particularly attractive part of Scotland's winter landscape.

STRA THSPEY RAILWAY CO. LTD.
SANTA SPECIAL
Wishing you a Merry Christmas.
4544

INDEX

PICTURE CREDITS

l = left; r = right; t = top;
b = bottom; m = middle

G Alliez: 109mr
Gordon V Allis: 39tr; 42b; 256
BJ Ashworth: 37t; 40b; 76b;
    128t
JH Aston: 52t
Paul Atterbury: 136m; 136bl;
    137t; 137mr; 137bl; 173t;
    173mr
Hugh Ballantyne: 12t; 174–5
RB Barr: 131ml
A Barrett: 35br
Philip Benham: 208t; 208b;
    209m; 209b
MN Bland: 88tr
RK Blencowe: 189t
John Bowers: 60t
Melvyn Bryan: 144b; 185t
DE Canning: 70t
Marion Canning: 176b
IS Carr: 182b,192t
Jim Carter: 41ml
HC Casserley: 129bl
RM Casserley: 16tl; 163tl
CRL Coles: 85tr; 114b; 179m
Richard J Cook: 31tl
Stanley Creer: 184b
Derek Cross: 198b
G Daniels: 179t
Hugh Davies: 124b
MEJ Deane: 177bl
HC Doyle: 36 ml
C Hamilton Ellis: 64b
TG Flanders: 17b; 197b
JA Fleming: 81br
JC Flemons: 118br
PR Foster: 190
PJ Fowler: 14 tr; 15t; 43bl;
    148tr; 192ml; 193b
C Gammell: 32t; 51b; 69ml;
    138–9; 148mr; 165b; 197t;
    234b; 237br; 244b
John Goss: 128b; 246
CC Green/HW Burman: 214t
D Griffiths: 32bl
David Haggar: 60b
FS Hall: 180t

L Hanson: 126t; 130tl; 237t
Tony Harden: 10m; 11t; 11l;
    11r; 11b; 12m; 12b; 13t; 13m;
    14tl; 14b; 17tr; 26tr; 26bl;
    27ml; 27br; 28tl; 28tr; 28m;
    29t; 29mr; 29bl; 29br; 30br;
    31tr; 36tr; 39tl; 43ml; 43mr;
    44tr; 44m; 44br; 45tl; 45mr;
    45bl; 45bm; 50br; 52bl; 53t;
    54b; 55t; 64ml; 66mr; 67bl;
    69bl; 71bl; 72tl; 74t; 74ml;
    74br; 76tr; 77tr; 78tr; 79bl;
    80mr; 86tl; 87tl; 87ml; 87b;
    90bl; 91ml; 95tr; 96ml; 97tr;
    97ml; 98t; 108ml; 111ml;
    112t; 112mr; 112bl; 113tr;
    113mr; 113b; 117mr; 117b;
    119ml; 121tl; 121m; 133t;
    140tr, 142tl; 144tr; 145mr;
    148b; 149b; 150m; 151t;
    151m; 151bl; 154ml; 154mr;
    156tr; 157t; 157m; 158b;
    164ml; 166ml; 166mr; 178tl;
    178mr; 179br; 181t; 187bl;
    193t; 193m; 199t; 199br;
    201t; 201mr; 203ml; 212tr;
    212b; 213t; 213b; 214tl;
    215br; 220tl; 220tr; 220ml;
    221tl; 221ml; 221mr; 221bl;
    221br; 228b; 229ml; 229br;
    230tr; 232tl; 232mr; 232b;
    233t; 233m; 234tr; 236br;
    237m; 240ml; 240mr; 240b;
    241tl; 241tr; 241m; 241b;
    242mr; 242bl; 245b; 248b
Ken Harris: 250t; 250b
JC Haydon: 50t; 53b; 54t; 244t
GT Heavyside: 129t; 200b
GF Heiron: 149t; 191b
Roger Holmes: 41tr
AC Ingram: 167b
E Ingram: 80tl
Alan A Jackson: 227b
AP & M Jacobs: 116b
HN James: 67br
Alan Jarvis: 2–3
Barry Jones: 65bl; 110; 189br
MA Jose: 126b
Justin Kerr-Peterson: 23tr

The Lordprice Collection
    (www.lordprice.co.uk): 46;
    46–7; 122; 160; 160–161;
    194; 194–195; 238; 238–239
Alan Meads: 23tl
Michael Mensing: 127t; 147b;
    184t
John H Meredith: 42mr
David Mitchell: 104b; 105t;
    105m; 105b
G Newall: 166tl
J Osgood: 125t; 187br
RB Parr: 242t
JA Peden: 109tl, 213mr
Paul Pettitt: 60–1m; 61br
Jenny Phillips: 172r; 173bl;
    173br
Hendy Pollock: 251t; 251m;
    251b
D Rendall: 18b
GA Richardson: 68m
Claire Rickson: 2ml; 23b
RC Riley: 82b; 98–9; 145b
Bill Roberton: 243b
Richard Salmon: 61bl
Eric Sawford: 38
John Scrace: 155b; 159
J Seagrim: 31b
WS Sellar: 146tl
NC Simmons: 97b
REB Siviter: 75
John Smallwood: 104–5m
Martin Snell: 22b
NE Stead: 203tr
JJ Stevens: 231b
K Taylor: 200t
Douglas Thompson: 163b;
    202t
Nigel Trotter: 209t;
Steve Turner: 196b
RE Vincent: 103b
Brian Webb: 219b
H Weston: 90t
HF Wheeler: 43tl
KW Wightman: 235b
JK Williams: 118t
E Wilmshurst: 205ml
Revd Graham B Wise: 108b
IL Wright: 95b

CHAPTER OPENER ILLUSTRATIONS

PAGES 24–5
*These Great Western Railway employees worked in various capacities
at Stourport station, in Worcestershire, in about 1900.*

PAGES 62–3
*Engineering teams, watched by plenty of casual spectators, are hard at work
replacing a bridge on a main line, probably in eastern England in the 1920s.*

PAGES 106–7
*Flanking their manager, a group of railwaymen pose in front of a new-looking
Hunslet locomotive on the Penrhyn Railway in Wales, in the early 1900s.*

PAGES 138–9
*In March 1959 a single passenger walks along the platform at Hawes station
to join the train to Garsdale, while the stationmaster waits to send the train away.*

PAGES 172–3
*In September 1956, The Fenman, a special organized by the Railway
Correspondence and Travel Society, took 310 enthusiasts in 15 open wagons
on a tour of Fenland branches.*

PAGES 210–11
*In August 1954, a Channel Islands boat train crosses Canute Road and enters
Southampton Docks, hauled by a Britannia Class locomotive, No. 70004,
'William Shakespeare'.*

AUTHOR'S ACKNOWLEDGEMENTS

The photographs used in this book have come from many sources. Some have been supplied by photographers or picture libraries, while others have been bought on the open market. In the latter case, whenever possible photographers or libraries have been acknowledged on page 255. However, many such images inevitably remain anonymous, despite attempts at identifying or tracing their origin. If photographs or images have been used without due credit or acknowledgement, despite our best efforts, apologies are offered. If you believe this is the case, please let us know, as we would like to give full credit in any future edition.

Life Along the Line is the sixth book in a series that started some years ago with *Branch Line Britain*, but it is the first to focus on the people who have always been at the heart of Britain's railway network. As a result this book, although clearly part of the series, has presented particular challenges in its planning, researching, writing and production. I owe a huge debt to everyone who has helped in this process. For assistance with research and the tracking down of unusual images, I am grateful to Tony Harden and Barry Jones, always generous with their knowledge and their collections, and to the many friends and enthusiasts I have met at railwayana and postcard fairs all over Britain. Charles Allenby and Julian Holland, with their remarkable knowledge of railway history, have been invaluable in checking proofs and correcting my many mistakes. Sue Gordon, patient, meticulous and always supportive, has been, as ever, the perfect editor, and Dawn Terrey the consummate designer. Thanks are also due to the staff of David & Charles, in particular Neil Baber, and to the staff of the following preserved railways: Bluebell, Churnet Valley, North Norfolk, North Yorkshire Moors, Strathspey, Talyllyn and West Somerset. Last but not least, I thank my wife Chrissie, who has not only survived, with patience, humour and equanimity, the long and demanding process of making yet another railway book, but has also, thanks to her computer skills, played a vital role in making the hundreds of ill-assorted images look their best.